The Disguised Guest

The
Disguised Guest

Rank, Role, and Identity
in the Odyssey

Douglas J. Stewart

Lewisburg
Bucknell University Press
London: Associated University Presses

© 1976 by Associated University Presses, Inc.

Associated University Presses, Inc.
Cranbury, New Jersey 08512

Associated University Presses
108 New Bond Street
London W1Y OQX, England

Library of Congress Cataloging in Publication Data

Stewart, Douglas J   1933–
The disguised guest.

Bibliography: p.
Includes index.
1. Homerus. Odyssea. 2. Homerus—Criticism and interpretation.
I. Title.
PA4167.S695   883'.01   74–18749
ISBN 0–8387–1647–4

Printed in the United States of America

For Walter J. Kropp

Contents

Preface

> Every scholar, once in his lifetime, wants to talk about
> Homer; no other scholar wants to listen to him.
>
> A. W. Gomme

FAIRNESS, TO READERS, TO REVIEWERS, AND TO MYSELF,
requires me to state at the outset that I am a nonspecialist
venturing into the highly specialized field of Homeric studies,
an area less and less trod by outsiders, because it has become
more and more technical and indeed almost mathematical.
Though I am a professional classicist, my areas of interest—social
and political thought, philosophy of history, and historiog-
raphy—are not generally thought to have a significant contribution to make to the present state of Homeric scholarship,
and indeed it is not often that one can find a study of Homeric
matters paying attention to the subjects I pursue in this book.
I think I understand the rueful sensations given expression
by Professor Gomme, the late and great commentator on
Thucydides, yet if I believed in his aphorism, I would not have
taken the trouble to collect my ideas about the *Odyssey*,
gathered from scattered class notes, public lectures, and mem-
oranda both to myself and colleagues, and do the work required
to turn my insights on the *Odyssey* into a book like this. On the
other hand, I confess to a brand of pessimism quite different
from that of Professor Gomme. Homeric scholarship, in addition
to being highly technical, is also frequently combative, and a
nonspecialist runs the risk of being challenged for trespass if he

barges into a restricted area. Unlike Professor Gomme, I occupy no eminence that requires that I be suffered silently, if not gladly, and there is every reason to expect that my words here *will* be noted and examined very carefully if they are not, in fact, charged with scholarly misdemeanor. Therefore, to avoid any possible misunderstandings, I must here present two preliminary points regarding the nature of this book and the arguments it makes; indeed, I am bound to do so, given the way in which Homeric scholarship generally by-passes the issues I treat here as central. (I treat them as central and for the purposes of this study; I say nothing of their centrality to the entire field of Homeric scholarship, nor am I urging that Homeric scholarship turn its attentions in this direction. I am simply saying that there are some interesting, if not astonishing, data in the *Odyssey,* read a certain way, that seem to yield a new frame and focus on its meaning.)

First, a plausible case can be made for a non-Homerist writing on the topics treated in this book, because, as was mentioned, Homeric scholarship has become intensely technical, and largely prescinds from questions about the meaning of the poems and/or their "intellectual" content, and thus a gap exists between the work of the professional Homerists who work on questions like the date, transmission, historicity, and composition of the Homeric poems and the field of pure literary criticism—a role also generally left to nonspecialists. My subject stands anonymously between the two. The reasons why professional Homerists do not normally deal with such matters as social ideology, psychology, class, rank, and role in the Homeric poems could hardly be explicated here, except to say that the history of classical scholarship, particularly with respect to Homer, has simply decreed otherwise. The almost simultaneous and contemporary eruptions of religious controversy and classical scholarship in sixteenth-century Europe were bound to have led, one might guess, to an approximation in the ways both the ancient scriptures and works of the ancient pagans were read and analyzed. The age that made Bible reading a grim duty was bound to make all other reading extremely dutiful as well. And as grim readers demand careful texts, editing was to become the most prized activity for both classical and biblical scholars. The close reading that editing demands led, in the case of Homer, to noticing all sorts of strange inconsistencies and oddities in the texts that do not usually figure even in the worst manuscripts of ancient authors who clearly *wrote* their works and maintained personal control over them until they were published, and all sorts of fanciful theories floated abroad about the nature of the compositional process that yielded the Homeric corpus, and then transmitted it through time to the earliest copyists whose handiworks we possess. (It is perhaps ironic that knowledge of the methods of composition and transmission of a particular *written* work is often vital to its editor, and that a search for parallel editorial answers in Homer led to the ultimate recognition that the Homeric poems were almost certainly *not* a written body of work and that very discovery was perhaps all too impressive to be entirely healthy.) With the rise of archaeolgy in the eighteenth and nineteenth centuries, attention widened to inquire into the historicity of the Homeric poems. Schliemann's discovery of Troy and excavation of Mycene produced both funds of evidence and guidelines of future activity on the possible historicity of the poems or their constituent details that are far from exhausting themselves to this day, with still more enthusiasm generated by every new discovery, and with discoveries now coming at an accelerating and almost predictable rate. Thus, the field of Homeric studies is understandably preoccupied with an enormous wealth of still only partly digested material. But meanwhile, what can the interested reader of Homer *today* expect to hear from the specialists on matters of theory or social attitude, or on problems about personal identity and social role, all of which he finds quite honestly in the texts of the poems?

Studies of the sort found in this book are going to come principally from outsiders. This book is the result, first, of a practicing teacher's experience with the *Odyssey,* while that teacher's *scholarly* preoccupations were attracted elsewhere. It was originally a pedagogical problem that began the process of reasoning and analysis. My previous scholarly interests lay in the area of social and political thought, broadly interpreted, and by a very natural process, I came to apply to the *Odyssey* categories of thought and mannerisms of doubt familiar enough in the areas where I normally work. I found a new way of interpreting the *Odyssey* as a poem rather tightly organized about the theme of dubious social rank or identity—of disguises—and therefore of confusion about personal worth and moral importance, which disguises would naturally cause.

This volume and its ideas originated not from a research project nor from traversing the usual scholarly haunts and pathways, but from the *ad hoc* demands of teaching and lecturing, both in the classroom and before public groups. Upon being asked to teach the *Odyssey,* I soon discovered that there is very little published material on the poem by Homeric scholars that is of any use for anyone considering it as literature, or indeed as a vehicle of ideas of any sort. This struck me as ironic. While Homerists have discussed the *Iliad* as a work of art, and other writers and critics need little urging to write commentaries on the *Iliad,* almost no one feels the urge to do so with the *Odyssey.* Yet writers, as distinct from scholars and critics, have always felt the pull of the *Odyssey* and many have engaged in reworkings of its basic mood and mechanisms, while they have almost universally ignored the *Iliad.* The year 1919 saw the completion of not just one modern classic retelling of the *Odyssey,* namely, Joyce's *Ulysses,* but also a second, Giraudoux's *Elpénor,* though the latter—a modest, slim work—was bowled over by the unfortunate coincidence and is now almost unknown and unread. Clearly writers have followed their instincts here, and have seen in the *Odyssey,* if not the greater Homeric poem, certainly the more useful one. That it should prove so useful to writers in particular seems to make a *prima facie* case that it is, and ought to be treated as, an important work of literature on which intelligible criticism can be done. Faced with the obligation of lecturing on the *Odyssey* as a poem, and lacking nearly all guidance from established authority, I tackled the task myself. At first it was only for class lectures and then for invited public lectures and seminars as a guest professor, and after a lot of persuasion, as a book-length text, which as I correctly foresaw took me away from the subjects I was originally more interested in. As time went on, I grew fascinated with the subject, and became more committed to my ideas and their fullest elaboration, and despite all too many setbacks and delays, I now have produced an expression of my ideas in the form I would have wanted them to appear. This text will provide future teachers and lecturers with basic grounds for critical analysis of the *Odyssey* that, for once, are not distracted by a greater eagerness to deal with the *Iliad,* the Homeric question, or ancient archaeology. The sole interest herein is the *Odyssey.*

Acknowledgments

I AM INDEBTED TO ALL THE STUDENTS WHO HAVE HEARD ME out on these ideas for the last ten years. (This volume, like the hero of the *Odyssey*, has taken just about a decade to reach its destination.) They originally offered me the challenge to find the important and the plausible in the *Odyssey* as literature; and their questions, criticisms, and written work have sent me back to the text again and again to discover a little more each time about the *Odyssey*. I am also very much indebted to two former Brandeis University colleagues, Professor Sacvan Bercovitch of Columbia University and Professor Martin Mueller of Brock University, who engaged me in long, intense, and congenial arguments about the nature of epic and the characteristics of the *Odyssey* in the years 1966 and 1967. I am thankful to Brandeis University for inviting me to lecture in the Adult Summer Institute in 1968, in which the theme was identity and individuality. In two lectures on the *Odyssey* (among the five I was asked to give) I discovered in their preparation more hard evidence to support my growing conviction that this was a key to the structure and much of the development of the poem. Subsequent lectures and courses each in turn added flesh to the basic scaffolding of my thesis. At the University of California at San Diego in 1970, where I taught the *Odyssey* in two different courses and also gave a departmental seminar on the poem, it was first suggested that I turn my ideas into a short book. Upon returning to Brandeis that fall, I began to take the suggestion more seriously and started work upon the volume soon thereafter.

15

A note on translation is due here. I have followed the Greek text of W. B. Stanford's edition of the *Odyssey* (St. Martin's Press, 1967), in making my own translations in the dullest of routine prose. I debated using published translations. But I found that every translator either suppresses, relocates, or understates some element in the sentence he is translating, and all too frequently it was that element in particular that was essential to the argument I was pursuing in a given case with a given text. Thus, the only possible resort was to make my own translations, which make no claim to literary finish, but only purport to be flat, accurate, and balanced rendering of *all* the elements that are in the Greek.

This book is affectionately and enthusiastically dedicated to Rev. Walter J. Kropp, SJ, who first taught me Greek at Loyola University of Los Angeles, and not just Greek but a certain independent and saucy irreverence for pomposity, along with a love for cleverness and wit. My wife, a Latinist whose field does not present such touchy problems as those connected with the Homeric epic, was remarkably supportive and encouraging throughout the long gestation period of this book, though remaining of the general opinion that Hellenists must be a bit "tetched," if they take this long to say their piece.

Introduction

THE THEME OF THE GUEST DISGUISED IS PERHAPS THE MOST unnoticed literary constant in the *Odyssey,* and is perhaps unnoticed because it is so constant. In events both portrayed and recounted (or invented, one may say), it appears as perhaps the key structural and operational device in the poem. Nearly all transitions from nonaction to action, from torpor and despair to aggressive action and hope, and vice versa, have to do with a disguised outsider and the enormous narrative energy released at the point of confrontation between bemused host and disguised guest. This is true even of remembered events preceding the action, especially those found in book 4; the Greeks inside the Wooden Horse were disguised guests of a sort, as was Menelaus disguised in a sealskin while lying in wait for Proteus. Athena is a disguised guest of Telemachus, twice, and Odysseus is in a sense disguised as the guest, first of the Cyclops and later of Circe, in that his false name constitutes a sort of disguise to the former, as does his drug-affected power to resist enchantments to the latter. His anonymity among the Phaeacians can be seen as another sort of disguise. And, finally, of course, Odysseus is a disguised guest in his own home—with an ironic twist or double-mirror effect, since as owner of the house invaded and provender wasted by the suitors, he is his own host, too. Moreover, it seems not altogether certain that Odysseus has a firm grasp on his own identity at this point.

This intense focus on guests, hosts, and uncomprehended identities seems to provide a prime clue to the poem's central motive force, a preoccupied concern with personal worth and

17

reality, which are first disguised by convention and social ritual,
and then further and doubly disguised by the narrative events
whenever people meet for all but the most trivial of social
purposes. Against this, one could set the typical practice of
heroic epic, in which apparent social rank, and therefore moral
worth, is always deducible from exterior tokens, such as dress or
appearance, even upon first meeting. The intrusion of disguises
into such a social situation would immediately destroy it, since
the typical world of heroic epic is, quite literally, a society
operating at face value.*

There seems to be an almost obsessive concern in the *Odyssey*
with what makes a man even know his own identity, when he
is stripped of conferred marks of social approval or disapproval
—which are natural and obvious in true heroic epic—since easy
recognition by others, using external tokens exclusively, has
become next to impossible in the poem. Why the *Odyssey,*
ostensibly an epic poem, should be so structured around a
conundrum about the central article of social faith held by an
epic-heroic society and the bulwark of its aristocratic values,
that is, the obviousness of moral worth as judged by social
position or personal appearance, is a question that is probably
impossible to answer. Nonetheless, the conundrum is there. The
Odyssey fundamentally challenges the social ideology of a heroic
class, and seems to be struggling to replace it with a different

---

* In the *Iliad,* appearance is everything, or an accompaniment of
everything. The commons are plain, if not outright ugly, and it is the
special sin of Thersites not just that he speaks contumaciously of Agamemnon, but that he does it being so frightfully ugly and low. As Homer
describes him (2.216 ff.), he is ugly, bald, so round-shouldered that his
shoulders meet before his collapsed chest, and bow-legged. The nobles,
on the other hand, are always represented as outstanding for some physical
feature, Achilles' looks, Agamemnon's height, or Odysseus' broadness of
shoulder (the latter two representing a neat trade-off in 3.166–69 and
192–94). In book 19, Achilles sadistically explains to Lycaon that the
latter can not realistically object to being murdered by himself because
he is far less handsome than Achilles and even Achilles has to die. Would
any hero of true epic consent to be disguised as Odysseus in book 12—as a
weak old man—simply to assure survival? The thought is absurd. Appearance is inseparable from reality in true heroic epic.

ideology, partaking of both peasant and middle-class values, though not limited to them, and indeed not terribly clear about what it considers an ideal substitute for the heroic model.

Naturally, the heroic conception of life exemplified by Achilles or Siegfried can occur as a reality in human consciousness and history only rarely, and can last only a brief time. It seems to grow out of, and just after, extremely warlike periods when whole peoples are in the flux of migration, doing battle almost to the point of extermination for sheer living space. Naturally there is a very high premium on extremely brave and powerful military heroes, like Achilles, Siegfried, or Roland, and naturally, too, they are expected to be somewhat unreflective. At the same time, and contrary to what we might expect, such periods present, at least in their epic retelling, not a slovenly and anarchic social system, but the opposite: a highly structured caste system, with elaborate and involuted ceremonials and courtesies serving in place of a more humdrum and citified body of *law,* the sort of thing that serves the periods of reflection and consolidation that follow an age of heroic exploit. (It may well be, of course, that the heroic frame of mind is not in fact contemporary with lives of such men who may be labeled heroes only after the fact by the tale-telling embroidery of those claiming to be their descendants.) Thus, while no one ever thought Homer in the *Iliad* was a contemporary of the events he described, one could ask whether Homer was fathering on his heroes an unreflectiveness about social status that bespeaks his own times, but not theirs necessarily. Yet again, one might ask, was Homer giving voice not to the true social thought of his own time or of Achilles' time but to some era in between? There are slight indications, from the tendency of primary epics to end with funerals and mourning, not so much for a man as for an age, that even heroic epic recognizes that the age it enshrines is gone, and in some sense preaches its valedictory. But that, as evidence, is perhaps more suggestive than conclusive. What is more concrete, and more central to the point here, is that the *Odyssey* is an epic that takes up after the funeral and concerns a sorrowing and tattered survivor of heroic society who has to learn how to function in a new and quite different world that has collectively forgotten heroism, except as history, and has acquired a new concern for the bourgeois values of stability and ease. (That the *Odyssey* is a postfunereal epic is heavily emphasized in the two Hades scenes, featuring Achilles and Agamemnon, and in the discussions of book 4 among Helen, Menelaus, and Telemachus—which dramatically represent the heroic age as over and dead.)

However the precise case may stand between a primary heroic epic like the *Iliad* and the social values it attributes to the world of the heroes, the *Odyssey* sits uncomfortably in the same genre with the *Iliad* because it deliberately questions the nature and validity of visible social rank, and in many given incidents seems to question rather specifically the authority of poems like the *Iliad,* and perhaps the *Iliad* itself, on these very matters. Here, perhaps, one example may serve for many. In book 11, the Underworld, the ghost of Achilles speaks bitterly of death and in response to Odysseus' rather formal and even unctuous tributes to his heroic career and glorious memory, he says with what could fairly be called a sob of remorse that he would rather serve as the hired hand of a tenant farmer, certainly as low a social position as Achilles could imagine, than reign as king over the "exhausted" dead. This passage is peculiarly bold, as well as crucial to the plot of the poem. It warns Odysseus not to expect to have both life and a continuation of his heroic career, like in the days of yore at Troy; and it prophesies the sort of life Odysseus will first experience on his return to Ithaca, living on the charity of Eumaeus, the pigkeeper. It also breaks to pieces the heroic attitude toward life, namely, that of Achilles in the *Iliad,* which demands that life must be of a certain quality or else it is insupportable. But, more cunningly and critically, it attacks the reigning motif of the poem we call the *Iliad* itself, not just the life choices of its hero, for the *Iliad* fully accepts as true and unquestionable Achilles' stated fate : to live either a short and glorious life, or a long and unhonored one. The *Odyssey,* in a passage like this, seems to say that Achilles either bequeathed to his poet, or was dealt by his poet, a false dilemma, which the career of Odysseus successfully eludes, saying that Odysseus will win great glory, and yet will attain long life, precisely because clinging to life at all costs, even at the cost of temporary humiliation, brings him through the very adventures that win him glory. And still closer to the point, it implies that the employment of disguises, which naturally deprive a hero of the right to insist on his glory and need of fame at every moment, will be part of Odysseus' fame when the accounts are finally settled, though the Homeric Achilles would not have borne the adoption of a disguise for a moment. It suggests, at least negatively, the idea that true glory and real greatness may not have much at all to do with the externals, tokens that meant everything to a hero like Achilles and, presumably, to his poet.

What there seems to be in the *Odyssey* is not another epic weakly imitative of the *Iliad,* but a counterepic, a long hexameter poem on a figure who begins his career as a true hero, but in his later actions is energetically engaged in nonheroic and even antiheroic actions just to stay alive. Yet this constitutes another and more genuine heroism. What this may say about the date of our poem may not be very important. On this sort of evidence, the poem must be later than the *Iliad* and by a different hand or hands. But that is not as significant as the fact that the *Odyssey* represents a contrasting, if not polemical, view of social reality as against the *Iliad,* and of the functioning personality within it. So, too, it seems to be of no great importance to ask whether the poet of the *Odyssey* is describing any actual social reality; and to the degree that his descriptions of social practices are argumentative, they must be seen as theoretical and ideal rather than either present or past reality. (The poet's demonstrable sympathy with people of humble station long ago generated the theory that the *Odyssey* is epic composed for peasants and in accordance with their thoughts. This might explain its differences with the *Iliad* as those of class difference rather than as evidence of historical change.)

This much being granted, is there anything in the *Odyssey,* as the threadbare modernism would have it, of a more positive character in respect to social attitudes? Probably not a great deal that could be called positive, or even that Hesiod might so characterize. Among the Greeks social reformism begins with Hesiod, not with Homer. There are elements of a more approved social code in the *Odyssey,* but they could be viewed as evidence of social regression rather than of reform or progress. The positive social recommendations of the *Odyssey* appear rather in the form of appeals to peasant morality, and even superstition. The most important contribution toward social betterment offered by the *Odyssey* is a strongly moralized reminder to its audience of the age-old Mediterranean superstition that gods travel about in shabby disguises, taking note of injustice, especially mistreatment of themselves, perpetrated by arrogant men who have no thought for tomorrow's vengeance. The gods then punish such men, whether simply because they have offended a god unknowingly or because the god chooses to represent all poor and lower-class victims of privileged arrogance. This moral theme is the substance of one suitor's anxious warning to his fellows in book 17, where it may mean no more than simple prudence. Hesiod, and the New Testament, despite their other great differences, share the view that divinity takes the special part of defenseless victims.[1]

But beyond this, there is very little of positive character in the way of recommendations for social betterment, not that this is particularly dismaying. The notion of social amelioration in antiquity was almost always accompanied by the idea of returning to more ancient and better conditions, which can be seen in Hesiod, Plato, and even Aristophanes.[2] If a distinct minority held a more progressivist or anthropological view of social issues,[3] they were still, without question, the exception. Second, however, it is important to note that a critique of unapproved social practices or values was, then as now, considered to be cogent and important in and for itself, well worth the effort involved. Social critics have no doubt always been embarrassed, and embarrassing, when challenged to present a positive program of reform to substantiate their eloquent and searching critiques (consider John the Baptist, vehemently preaching reform, but reduced to a rather jejune list of mild rights and wrongs when asked by his hearers for specific advice on how to carry out the particulars of reform[4]—though in all fairness, one must note that people who listen respectfully to social reformers are usually unoffending people in no great need of reform).

Finally, there is a reflective—or reflexive—character to the *Odyssey* that we do not find in the *Iliad*. The *Odyssey* in some sense seems to know itself *as* a poem, a literary creation or artifact. Assuming that a neutral legend of Odysseus preceded the formation of the poem, it appears that at some point in the process an introspective moment occurred and one or many poets discovered the existence of truly literary themes latent in the legend. At that point, a kind of editorial revision was decreed whereby the poem was rearranged, episodes recatalogued, and the point of view reworked—all to bring into plain view, to the fullest possible degree, the presence of literary skills at work in the poem, if not indeed to redirect the attention of an audience away from the raw events of the tale and toward the cunning devices of presentation and control exercised in the telling and by the teller. "Literary" is used here to mean a new attention toward plot control, devices, themes as themes, and authorial pride. The largest single literary maneuver was, of course, to build the theme of the disguised guest and make it the chief organizing idea of the piece.

But, having achieved this sort of maneuver, the poet was unlikely to fall back into the anonymity of the oral poets, illiterate and anonymous bards[5] who created the *Iliad*; and thus any number of devices and tricks are employed to keep the fact of the poet's achievements before our eyes, and not just the achievements themselves, but the figure of the poet himself. First, there is the obvious fact that poets play a part in the poem as characters, and as honored and trustworthy characters, too. More important, though somewhat less obvious, if *Iliad* and *Odyssey* are contrasted, poets fill a serious social and intellectual vacuum left behind by priests, who disappear entirely from the poem, as does almost all religion : except for one or two perfunctory sacrifices performed by Odysseus and his men, the one broadly staged act of religion is the lordly sacrifice of Nestor in book 3 (Nestor is a fairly obvious fossil remnant of another age). There is as well, a near-vacuum left behind by soothsayers, only two of whom appear in the *Odyssey* : Theoclymenus, who is a failure, and Teirisias, who is dead and is not introduced to predict the future in any case, but to give directions and report on the past.

More subtle, and even more important, is the fact that the construction of the poem at several places reminds us that a poet and his tactical decisions are in control of the way we are permitted to hear the tale. Odysseus' rhetorical question to himself at the opening of book 9—shall I tell my tale front-to-back or back-to-front?—at one level constitutes a rather daring identification on the poet's part between himself and his craft on the one hand, and his hero, because it is a literary question, a poet's question; at another level, however, it reminds the cannier members of an audience that a poet is not governed by the mere rush of events nor is he bound to tell them as they occurred, or as the Muse declares them, but he can pick and choose, and invert the order of episodes if he should prefer, for purposes that could only be called rhetorical or artistic, if those terms are permitted to describe the consciousness of a poet or poets working so early in the history of literature. I think we can and must do that here. This conception of a poet's scope and freedom is not something to be found in the *Iliad* or primary epic in general. But, if Odysseus' literary rhetorical question is considered further, a realization is possible that the question of what sequence a narration should follow reflects directly on the state of the poem as it is up to the time Odysseus speaks. The strategy followed in the first eight books by the poet has in fact been to deploy the narration of events back-to-front; he has told that much of the tale of Odysseus tail-end foremost. (Also notable is the fact that Odysseus, despite his conventionally complimentary words about the Muse of the Phaeacian poet Demodocus a few moments before, does not himself invoke any Muse, nor even his own memory, which one might say was the natural substitute for a Muse in the case of a first-person, eye-witness account of events, but rather he seems either to possess all the facts without effort. Or—given his status as a fabricator[6] —he is consulting his imagination! But in either case, the observation is justified that his concern is with effect, cogency, and, no doubt, the good will of his audience, all of which result in a question of taste and free will, perhaps the two concepts most fundamental to the idea of individual art and artistry.)

But most important of all, the poet or poets of the *Odyssey*, having discovered literature as it were, seem eager for recognition and praise for their ability to conceive and maintain a plot, a consistent and convergent pattern of actions leading to a conclusion that is not just the terminal point of a well-known legend, in this case the happy reconciliation of Odysseus and Penelope, but a true denouement in the strict sense of a well-constructed drama, an ending adequately motivated and causally linked to all that has gone before. It is my particular concern in chapter 3 to illustrate how the complex details of the reconciliation between Odysseus and Penelope, long dragged out and neurotically devious, make little sense unless they are seen as proceeding, step by step, from all the events of the earlier books that have shaped Odysseus' character, making him pathologically cautious, and inward and roundabout—a parody as it were of his general (and quite a bit older) reputation for scheming—and the construction of this sort of effective and satisfactory plot is the occasion of the utmost pride in its creator.

The preoccupation with plot in the mind of the poet of the *Odyssey* may also contribute to some of the inconsistencies of the *Odyssey*, which are often thought to be more tremendous than those of the *Iliad*. It seems likely, first, that there were preceding the *Odyssey* one or more neutral poetized legends of Odysseus, giving at least a catalogue of his adventures, in straight-forward chronological order, along the lines of the narrative chronology of the *Iliad*.[7] This version, or these versions, was or were considerably reworked by the poet to produce a very different thing indeed, the extant *Odyssey,* with its breathtakingly complex time sequence, its converging lines of plot, with respect to the psychological state of the hero, and the aforementioned social and cultural preoccupations. But this meant, given a poetic determination to rearrange episodes from earlier and perhaps competing versions of Odysseus' life by reorienting them toward a prethought conclusion, that some violence would be done to the raw materials, that is, the pre-existing bardic materials were forced into the frame of a plot based on a new concept of literary organization, and inevitably, like ill-fitting stones forced into a mosaic for which they were never originally prepared, some of their edges became chipped and frayed in the process. Such problems are particularly acute, especially in book 8, where two quite different and conflicting descriptions of the life and habits of the Cyclopes are given, and in book 11, where the real purpose of the trip to the underworld is in some doubt, given the obvious collapse of its stated purpose, which then tempts one to speculate what the episode means: why book 11 was left as it is, despite the glaring inconsistencies, where it joins the rest of the fabric of the poem, unless more was seen to be gained than lost by this inclusion. In both cases certain kinds of inconsistency are tolerable to this poet in return for certain contributions the episodes make to the general forward thrust of the newly discovered use of plot.

As noted, Odysseus prevails over Circe's enchanting drugs by means of a counterdrug, called *moly* by Homer and given him by Hermes. The twentieth century has perhaps the first one in thousands of years that is quite prepared to accept the fact, though it has always been present, that the *Odyssey* is one of the very few works of respectable literature that acknowledges the power of drugs and seems to accept the existence of drugs by consenting to describe their effects, not just personal but social, without wincing or disapproving. Drugs, in some cases in the *Odyssey*, affect not just consciousness, but notions of identity and/or the sense of social reality. Drugs are surely crucial in book 4, in the Circe episode and where Helen doctors the drinks of Menalaus, Telemachus, and the others so that remembering past injuries will not provoke new angers. Drugs are at least present and interesting in the incident of the Lotus Eaters. Drugs are possible in the case of the strange wine Odysseus gives the Cyclops. And drugs are conceivably involved in strange ways with the fantastic cosmography of book 11, which is perhaps more closely connected with the Circe episode than has been suspected. A record of the point reached in my research is offered in the appendix, because, at least in some cases, it has a bearing on the main theme of this volume.

Notes

1. Compare Hesiod, *Works and Days,* lines 5–8 : "Easily he makes strong, and easily he brings the strong man low; easily he humbles the proud and raises the obscure, and easily he straightens the crooked and blasts the proud—Zeus who thunders aloft and has his dwelling on high," with the triumphant song of Mary in Luke 1.52ff. : "He has hurled down the mighty from their thrones and raised up the lowly. He has filled the wretched with good things, and has sent the rich away empty. . . ." (Translation of Hesiod by H. D. Evelyn-White, in *Hesiod, Homeric Hymns, Homerica,* The Loeb Classical Library [London, 1954].) The Greek notion is that the gods are capricious in dealing with men—though Hesiod finds even this an opportunity to warn of the need for justice; while the Hebrew notion is that God is systematically hostile to the great and powerful, though nations are probably more to the fore in the chant of Mary than individuals

2. *See* Hesiod's express desire to have been born either before or after his own day in the Age of Iron (*W & D* 174–75), and indeed his confidence that society in the future would return to the conditions of the Golden Age is quite limited. Clearly the earlier age was the better. This idea is taken up in Plato *Republic* 2. 372–74, 3. 414 (The Noble Lie passage, echoed in 8. 546 ff., where the Noble Lie is finally admitted to be Hesiodic). See also the same general idea in Aristophanes *Birds* 481 ff.

3. *See* E. A. Havelock, *The Liberal Temper in Greek Politics* (New Haven and London: Yale Univ. Press, 1964), pp. 5–8 and chapters 2 and 3.

4. *See* Luke 3. 11–14. The man with two cloaks should give one away to someone more needy than he; tax-farmers should take no more than their quotas; and soldiers were to avoid civil rumpus and be satisfied with their pay.

5. *See* Milman Parry, *The Making of Homeric Verse,* ed. A. Parry (Oxford: Oxford Univ. Press, 1971) and A. B. Lord, *The Singer of Tales* (New York: Athenaeum Press, 1968), chs. 5–7.

6. *See* C. R. Beye, *The Iliad, The Odyssey and the Epic Tradition* (New York: Doubleday & Co., 1966), p. 184.

7. *See* W. J. Woodhouse, *The Composition of Homer's Odyssey* (Oxford: Oxford Univ. Press, 1930), esp. ch. 19.

The Disguised Guest

Every scholar, once in his lifetime,
wants to talk about Homer; no other scholar
wants to listen to him.

A. W. Gomme

1

Odysseus and the Cyclops:
The Heroic Code
Reviewed ... and Rejected

IN BOOK 9 OF THE *ODYSSEY* TIME IS BENT BACK UPON ITSELF
and the pressure is so intense and violent that time itself seems
nearly to snap in two. Odysseus here for the first time identifies
himself to his hosts, the Phaeacians of the Island of Scheria. As
he begins to tell the tale of his wanderings up to this moment,
he says:

> I am Odysseus, son of Laertes, I who exceed all men in
> tricks, and my fame reaches heaven. I dwell in sunny Ithaca.

There is irony latent in every word. The hero's fame may indeed
reach the heavens—Demodocus the bard had sung of Odysseus
earlier, in the very presence of the then unnamed hero—but
it now appears to be detached from the person of the vag-
abond-hero, who must in fact identify himself to his unsus-
pecting hearers and hosts, as they naturally have no idea who
he is. He is the guest disguised by both anonymity and estrang-
ing distance, if not by the very fact of his status as a hero of the
past! (If the bard Demodocus knows his tale, he is virtually
history and thus unreal!) Another irony resides in the fact that
Odysseus has dwelt, if dwelling is the word to use, everywhere

but Ithaca for the previous ten years—indeed there arises some suspicion that his absence from his home, and not just his home, but nearly all civilized society, has effectively changed his character, and he may or may not really be Odysseus any longer. Finally, there is the irony that this opening would have made a useful, and typical, opening of a respectable epic poem devoted to the adventures of Odysseus returning home—which might have taken two or three years.[1] But appearing where it does, almost at the center of an epic that is told backwards, it creates the odd effect of suggesting that identity and names are very fragile and fleeting things in the world of this poem, and are something less than we take them to be.*

Book 9 is also the place where Odysseus, in telling his tale, has *last* used his own name, in the tale of the Cyclops. Though both utterances occur in the same book (backwards) they are chronologically ten years apart, and between these two occurrences Odysseus' name is never pronounced by his own lips, insofar as the *Odyssey* itself tells the tale. The poem throws this into the full glare of attention at two points. When Odysseus

---

* Judging by the practice of Homer in the *Iliad* and Virgil in the *Aeneid,* scholars in antiquity laid down the law that an epic must begin *in medias res,* plunging into the action when it is well under way. The opening of book 9 of the *Odyssey* might fit this "law," but not the actual beginning at book 1 we have in our version of the poem, which might be said to begin rather *vacuis in rebus,* in stagnation, inaction, and torpor. This is but one example of the way the *Odyssey* as we have it seems to go out of its way to challenge standard epic practice, assuming that the *Iliad* represents more standard practice, in this instance with time trickery. The effect hoped for, if not always produced, was, one suspects, to impress an audience with a shift in mode from epics like the *Iliad.* In the *Iliad,* action-*cum*-danger or grand ceremonial occasions are the only possible venues for major episodes; book 1 of the *Iliad* opens with a mixed scene involving both. In the *Odyssey,* which opens with debate among gods and confused inaction among men, and with its hero missing, talk has replaced most action, danger has been replaced, mostly, by boredom, and grand ceremonial occasions—like the banquet of the Phaeacians—have been turned into tricky social puzzles and misidentifications. The openings of either book 9 or book 5 (Odysseus leaving Calypso on his raft), would have made more typical and plausible epic openings than the actual opening we have.

mets Circe on the isle of Aeaea, and again when he meets Teirisias in the Underworld, on both occasions these figures immediately identify him and address him as though they had known him all his life.

> CIRCE : You are surely Odysseus, man of many vicissitudes
> (10.330)
> TEIRISIAS : Godlike son of Laertes, resourceful Odysseus
> (11.92)

Odysseus had never met either of them, and so it is odd that they know him, first of all, and second, it is odder that they should address him in these particular formulaic terms, since they are, as it were, the key epithets by which Odysseus was first described in the poem. Circe's *polytropos* ("man of many vicissitudes") in fact quotes the first line of the *Odyssey;* and Teirisias' *polymechane* ("resourceful") is probably the most common epithet in the poem for Odysseus. It might seem wholly appropriate that Circe, a goddess, and Teirisias, the one man whose ghost is supposed to retain intelligence in Hades, logically—or theologically—should very well know Odysseus' identity. But that sort of mechanical reasoning misses the point of such passages, where the question is not what powers such super-human characters technically have, but why Odysseus so amazingly fails to deliver his own introductions, and why they, whatever their powers, so fail in epic courtesy as to prevent him doing so. Especially since names and identities are crucial in epic poems, because epic heroes normally cannot function or bear to go without formulaic self-identification in every interview with another figure of any importance. What we need by way of explaining this lack of self-identification on the part of Odysseus, is not a disquisition on the supernatural powers of Circe or Teirisias, but really an answer to the question, why Odysseus fails to identify himself. Why, we and the reader must ask, has the poet so staged these scenes that other characters (whatever their metaphysical status) are willing, and not just able, to forestall the hero and make his own introductions for him? What is going on? Why has the poet denied Odysseus the right to introduce himself with patronymic, epithet, and homeland, just as he does later in the court of the Phaeacians? This was a right most jealously guarded in societies portrayed by heroic epic.

Clearly the poet wanted to *avoid* having Odysseu mention his own name, and thus makes Circe and Teirisias rush in to relieve him of that social obligation. And why should this be? Epic heroes normally like nothing better than reciting their pedigree, achievements, and homeland, on any and all occasions. It is done constantly in the *Iliad*. Why is Odysseus denied this pleasurable and indeed socially necessary activity?

The answer appears to be that the poet does not want Odysseus to name himself for the simple reason that he is somehow not himself. My argument is that in his wanderings Odysseus has become not simply a "different person"—as one might speak of a character in a novel—but a nonperson. His misfortune, at the beginning of his adventures with the Cyclops, began a process that actually amounts to the destruction of Odysseus the epic hero —it literally destroys him without quite killing him—and the rest of the wanderings complete the job. The second half of the poem, then, really becomes the story of a man devising a new personality because he has lost his old identity and is forced to think of who he now is—a task the heroes of standard epic could not have faced. In other words, the *Odyssey* is fundamentally the story of a survivor from a heroic age who outlives that age and must be taught how to function in a new society that has no conversance with or direct sympathy for what has passed. The poem is an account of the moral reeducation of an epic hero into an entirely new kind of role and vocation. That education begins like thunder with the adventure of the Cyclops.

The story of Odysseus and the Cyclops is probably the best-known non-Biblical story in all of Western culture and history. It is certainly the best-known Greek story, to people who know little of the *Odyssey* itself or any other Greek literature. This is obviously because it is a very good story. It appears to survive transplantation. Actually it is a story thousands of years old, older than the *Odyssey* by a great deal, for it is not an epic tale at all, but a folktale, the sort of tale that can and has been told in any and all societies, and with everybody and nobody as its hero. The first full and open break with epic materials and conventions in the poem is the decision of the poet to plunge his hero into folktales, and the first of them is not so very different from the tale of "Jack and the Beanstalk." Thus this tale—and by "this tale" I mean both its folklorish ancestry as well as its particular treatment in the *Odyssey*—could be taken boldly into the twenty-first century by Clarke and Kubrick in the hit, science-fiction movie of 1968, *2001: A Space Odyssey*. In the movie, "HAL," the madly malevolent computer with its great glowing red eye, is obviously a space-age, electronic Cyclops from which the hero, like Odysseus, can only escape by strategem and daring. And when he begins to disconnect the computer's circuits one by one, we are simply seeing one more version of the timeless story wherein a poor weak human being employing concentration—Odyssean cunning or modern science, it makes little difference—first makes drunk and then blinds a powerful and inhuman monster in order to escape him. (It was the computer's drunken singing—"Daisy, Daisy"—and generally inchoherent speech followed by the burning out of its red electronic "eye" that first alerted me to this parallel.) This is apt enough illustration that the basic material of the story, then, falls into the category of folktale : it is something rooted in no particular time and place, but transportable into any and all cultures, and capable of being retold in a thousand disguises.[2]

But what is a folktale doing in the midst of an epic? The epic is normally thought to be so firmly rooted in its own time and space (or in two times : that of the events themselves and that of the telling) as to constitute a fossil remnant of bygone cultures even before it is quite properly finished. Yet the *Odyssey,* though it is of epic length, contains a great deal of folk material, especially in the books of the Wanderings, books

9 through 12. Is it likely that this intrusion appears solely to vary the pace or to entertain those more easily bored in the poet's audience? That hardly seems likely, especially since the tales seem to fit a dominant social and moral ideology so well. (And, again, if the tales were chosen simply for entertainment, one would think they would have been scattered more evenly up and down the length of the poem.) No, the tales are not inimical to the overall plan of the *Odyssey*, whatever their origin, even though they should be *if* the poem were a conventional epic. Indeed they seem carefully chosen to promote and support the operation of the theme of the alienated guest.

A prior puzzle of the *Odyssey*, however, stems from the fact that the poem begins minus its hero. He is totally absent from the first four books, while we follow his adolescent son's intricate dealings with a situation that is socially, politically, and morally bewildering, to him and to the reader. Then again there is the strange business of books 5–8 where Odysseus is finally introduced at the end of his journeys, and one is more than a little confused by his strangely world-weary and cynical mood. (It is puzzling if the story is followed in the order the poet tells it: something of narrative power and finesse is lost because most people already know of the Wanderings of books 9–11 *before* and can not help anticipating more than the poet seems to have intended here because a combination of the poet's skill and the folk origins of these tales made these particular stories too popular and too elusive to remain strictly *his*. As the ages wore on, these tales escaped the total frame of the *Odyssey* to take up an independent life of their own. Or perhaps it is better to say that they returned to their place of origin—folklore, which knows no literary or political boundaries—and took Odysseus with them. In any case, the poet's procedure, here, however we account for its origins, seems a strange way to tell an epic story, backwards and sideways at once.

By the time the reader reaches book 9, he finally begins to follow Odysseus on his adventures—which, though they are past and recollected adventures, and partly folklore, are still active and energetic in a way at least loosely similar to the action of a more traditional epic like the *Iliad*. The first eight books of this singular epic were all talk and debate, except for the little bit of Conrad-like typhoon-writing at the end of book 8, which gets Odysseus from Calypso's isle to Scheria. The first important adventure Odysseus recounts after the lesser matters of trying to sack the city of the Cicones, and the Lotus Eaters, is that on the isle of the Cyclops, which returns to the ages-old motif of a weak human being trapped by his own curiosity in the lair of a murderous cannibal of gigantic size—or some other form of nonhuman power—and the story of how he escapes through the use of wit and trickery.

The interesting thing about the story, however, is in its finale, or its epilogue; for the one element in the story that most certainly does not come from the world of folktale is the temptation to which Odysseus succumbs at the end. Though he has blinded Polyphemus and has not only escaped from the cave, but also made off with many of the giant's sheep and then put safely out to sea, Odysseus simply can not accept his rare good luck and leave well enough alone. He can not resist suddenly shouting an insult at the monster, who thereupon almost destroys the ship with a well-thrown boulder, guided merely by the sound of Odysseus' voice. Not even intimidated thereby, or even particularly satisfied, Odysseus shouts out yet again :

> Cyclops, if some mortal should ever ask the name of him who shamed and blinded you, say it was Odysseus beseiger of cities who did it, the son of Laertes who dwells on Ithaca.
> (9.502–505)

This sort of thing is simply "not done" in folktale; folk heroes are humble and pragmatic. In fact, they are almost always poor and insignificant people and their victories are triumphs of peasant cunning, or thoughtless innocence, but hardly of aristocratic chivalry. Having escaped from the giant (or the witch, or the devil, or whatever) they go quietly about their business and do not ask for trouble with unnecessary challenges directed toward dangerous monsters. Odysseus is, however, an epic hero caught up in what is essentially a folktale, the rules of which he is hardly equipped to understand. First, he nearly has his ships sunk for his bravado in saying anything to Polyphemus once he has consummated his escape, and then, still worse, he reveals his real name to Polyphemus so that the giant can put it into a curse that the god Poseidon will ratify. And from what we can tell of the art, or science, of cursing, curses have no effect unless and until the correct name is employed.[3] In ancient Greece, you could not, as it were, make out a curse : To whom it may concern. . . . This fact is emphasized by the words of the giant himself a few lines further on :

> Hear me, Poseidon, earth-shaker of the blue locks. If I am truly yours, if you claim to be my sire, grant that Odysseus the city-beseiger may never return home—I mean the son of Laertes, who dwells on Ithaca.

> (9.528–31)

The quotation is too exact—and the sense of afterthought, of putting the finishing touches on in the last line, is too strong to allow any other inference : it was Odysseus' own ill-advised revelation of his name, pedigree, and epithet that permitted the monster to put them into a curse that will pursue him for ten long and ghastly years. Presumably Odysseus knew the rules for cursing as well as anyone else in his time, so why then did he take such a risk?

Here a brief comparison with the *Iliad* is instructive. It seems reasonably clear that the *Iliad* is the earlier poem of the two, for the *Odyssey* poet appears to know the *Iliad* and not vice versa. But the *Odyssey* seems later not just in date of composition but on a more profound level, in the age of moral and social attitudes that it embodies. It seems to be an obvious attempt to move away from the social conventions and standards of behavior found uncriticized in the older poem—sometimes to quarrel directly with those conventions and standards, and sometimes just to put ironic distance between itself and them for purposes of study. The basic cause of outright quarrel seems to be the *Odyssey* poet's loud insistence, in flat contradiction of the *Iliad,* that men have moral responsibilities they cannot shirk, and that human society is held together by the fact that human acts have foreseeable and proportionate consequences, and, except in rare cases, the capricious interference of the gods in human affairs cannot seriously affect men's fates. Neither proposition is true of the society pictured in the *Iliad,* while the *Odyssey* is opened and closed by scenes underscoring these very points: Zeus' proclamation in book 1 that Aegisthus deserved his fate because he knew beforehand what would come of his actions, and the punishment of the suitors and handmaidens at the end because they too had been warned (against committing nearly the same crime as Aegisthus) and had made light of that foreknowledge. On matters less cosmic, it would appear that the *Odyssey* poet contradicts the *Iliad* less than he smirks or mocks at it, which is more specifically to my point here. In the older poem we find that to proclaim one's prowess and pedigree was a standard and cherished item of heroic behavior, both socially useful and diplomatically seemly on almost every possible public occasion. And so in reciting his dossier to the Cyclops, Odysseus is very much in character as an epic hero who might be at home in the *Iliad.* It was expected of the epic hero that he would take intense verbal pleasure in such a recital—if he did not, who would? Of course the nonepic circumstances here undermine such heroic conventions, and constitute the almost fatal irony of the episode. As such, they are thus a key to the first half of the poem. What happens when the complicated conventions of a heroic code, embodied in a typically uncritical epic hero, clash with a world that knows, literally, nothing of any social convention at all? How does a hero survive in a new world and a new age that is none of his making or even of his imagining, an age than can neither believe in heroes, nor, in this case, tolerate their presence!

On the other hand this particular convention was more

than a matter of mere pleasure and prerogative for the authentic epic hero. The epic equivalent of the modern passport and letter of credit was the formulaic set-speech identifying oneself by pedigree, place of origin, and a formula that encapsulated one's most important achievements—city-beseiger, for instance. The identity of a man in heroic society was bound up with this kind of self-proclamation. These three factors gave Odysseus, or any hero, his public being, his claim to recognition. A man who has lost the opportunity—or the right—to delineate his own being in this way had almost ceased to exist. That is an unquestioned assumption in the *Iliad*. The classic example of this social fact of life is that intriguing cameo scene in *Iliad*, book 6, where Diomedes and Glaucus break off a duel to go through an elaborate ritual of self-identification, replete with endless dissertations on their respective family histories. It happens that their families were connected by ties of special friendship and hospitality going back many generations, and so they agree to part friends, and to avoid one another in battle henceforth, in order not to violate this special relationship—which transcends politics and the requirements of strategy—by trying to kill each other. (To be realistic, one could express wonder that it took ten years of the war for Glaucus and Diomedes to come across one another and discover this old connection. But of course realism has nothing to do with this sort of scene in epic narrative.

The epic technique of the *Iliad* is aimed, at least in part, not toward telling a story directly, but toward giving a panoramic and valedictory view of the heroic era and its social usages—as though to pay them tribute because they are regarded as now past and unrecoverable, a point made more explicit in the written imitation of epic, *Beowulf*.[4]) Nor was it just a matter of one's self-identification. As other passages of the *Iliad* indicate, the ritual of naming by pedigree and honors was needed to address others as well: it was one important item of that system of etiquette that quite literally seems to have held heroic society together and allowed it to function in spite of the near-total political and moral anarchy that we see pervading the heroic society of the *Iliad*.* If in the *Odyssey* we see society moving toward concepts of property, responsibility, and law, one can say that it is moving away from the society pictured in the *Iliad*, which is ruled almost solely by concepts of courtesy and honor. For instance, Nestor—in the course of a speech about something else entirely, as is his wont—stops to remark how important it is for a man of affairs to have at his fingertips a knowledge of the pedigree and accomplishments of all his social and political peers, and singles out for special praise the young king Peleus, who had acquired this knowledge within early youth and with a special sense of responsibility.[5] There are indeed times when this preoccupation seems nearly grotesque to us. In book 10 of the *Iliad*, Agamemnon at one point is telling Menelaus to go gather the Greek captains for a conference: it is nighttime and the Greeks are in trouble; Hector has been pressing them all day and now has them bottled up hiding behind a palisade built to protect their beachhead and their ships. Then Agamemnon adds that Nestor is to accompany Menelaus and check on the sentries as they make their rounds, to make sure they are awake on this dangerous night. Then, this order is given:

> Call out to each man you approach and wake him up, addressing each by his father's name and lineage, and listing his full honors: do not be too proud for this—it is our burden; as indeed Zeus seems to have chosen us for nothing but burdens since our birth.

> (10.67–71)

* Anarchy, in our terms at least. On the political side, consider the actual political condition existing among the Greeks before Troy: despite Odysseus' speech in book 1 insisting on the rights of monarchy, Agamemnon's authority is something less than clear or all-powerful, for though he can apparently take away Achilles' prize, he cannot force Achilles to continue fighting, or even discipline Diomedes for insulting him and his prowess. On the moral side virtually no one in the tale will or can admit that their actions are their own responsibility, from Paris' denial that his amour, that has gotten Troy into an astounding political situation, is really his responsibility, to Helen's demonstrated inability to fight Aphrodite, to Agamemnon's cool assertion that his alienation of Achilles wasn't really his fault, but the result of the working of some evil power.

Thus, despite his mood, the hour, the occasion, and its dangers
—though all this palaver will surely delay the supposedly urgent
conference and might even increase their danger—Agamemnon
dares not neglect, in the interest of efficiency, the fragile verbal
links that keep his society in one piece. (In fact the conference
turns out not to be urgent, for conferences rarely settle matters
in the *Iliad,* but worsen them.)

Odysseus began his literary career as an epic hero in the
Iliad, of course. And so it is only natural that even in the later
poem he too should feel the strength of his tradition's social
constraints, and despite the danger in this situation, where the
enemy is not an epic character but a nonsocial being with no
etiquette or formalities to observe, and in the face of his crew's
objections that when dealing with outraged giants, silence is
saftey—despite all this he feels compelled to proclaim himself
to Polyphemus by name, title, homeland, paternity. Though it
was folly, it was natural: it obviously makes Odysseus feel
familiar with himself again. But it was more than natural; it
was compensation for wounded feelings.

While a prisoner in the cave of the Cyclops, Odysseus, the
great tactician and sacker of cities and king (more or less) of
Ithaca, had been forced to use a tactic humiliating indeed to
an epic hero. He had been forced to call himself "nobody" or
"no man" (9.336–37) in order to deceive the giant and eventually gain his freedom. Strictly speaking, of course, he had used
the device without, at the time, really knowing what use it would
be to him—it was only an accident that made it useful. But
even though it turned out to be a lifesaving strategem, it still
rankled. In the code of heroes it was tantamount to social
suicide for one to deny his being and his name, to suppress his
list of noble deeds, even in moments of great urgency or danger,
as can be seen in the passage in *Iliad* book 5. And indeed it
was precisely at moments of great danger that such a proclamation was most desirable and important, for in those moments
one found the greatest possibility of glory, when danger was
great and all the witnesses knew exactly who you were, so that

your success, if you were successful in surmounting danger, was entirely yours. Pronouncing one's name and accomplishments served as the proper formula for a challenge prior to combat, just so that one's own glory would result. Here, *after* combat —which makes it sound lame and even slightly comic—and after a combat that was not exactly heroic combat, Odysseus is trying to salvage a poor second-best, and even that turns into just more trouble. (Nor was it just that he called himself nobody, but that he had gotten himself involved in a folktale, and in folktales the heroes are usually people of no importance, and certainly of no historical dimensions—if they have names at all they only have first names, like Jack or Cinderella—and Odysseus has gotten himself involved in an adventure with no witnesses who are his peers, which, besides, his peers might have some trouble crediting, not just because of the fabulous side of the tale, but because the loutish Cyclops was anything but a proper aristocratic opponent.) In the *Iliad* one cannot imagine a hero reneging on the chance to proclaim his identity to a stranger, friend, foe, or neutral, no matter what the risks. Such self-denial would hardly have appeared to an Iliadic hero as a real choice at all, since the denial of the self, even for a moment and for tactical reasons, was worse than death. And so Odysseus, on the point of escaping scot-free, can not contain himself and against all prudence shouts his name to Polyphemus. Guided by the sound—and being totally immune to heroic customs and verbal rituals—the monster first nearly capsizes the ships with a well-aimed boulder and then hurls an even more effective weapon, the curse that scuttles Odysseus' hopes for ten years.

Such is the answer of mere nature to the elaborate artificialities of the heroic code. Odysseus' shouted resumé, with name, pedigree, and deeds, was the last gasp of that code, and the rest of his story is basically a tale of the hero's reconstruction of a new life out of the ruins of a dead concept of the heroic figure. And Polyphemus' boulder becomes one of the more significant milestones in the history of social thought.

It has been stated that Odysseus is a survivor from a heroic age who outlives that age and must be taught how to function in a new society. The poet of the *Odyssey* has detached Odysseus from his accustomed environment and forced him through a series of appalling scrapes and boring delays so that he may find within himself a new and individualized reason for being—since nothing else is left to him by way of support and resource. Of course Odysseus fights the process almost every step of the way, but he survives and triumphs because, paradoxically, he has learned to yield. Throughout the Adventures, one has a gathering impression that it is the poet, or the poetic mind, representing one or more individuals, even more than the curse, that is literally forcing the hero through events, a planning intelligence half-inside and half-outside the action, which in a sense plots against the hero's self-conscious intentions in order to make a better and more believable man of him.

Structurally, the *Odyssey* follows a much more complicated pattern than the *Iliad,* a complexity in which the poet takes deep professional satisfaction. It opens with a displaced hero, lost somewhere off the edge of the map, while his son, the rawest kind of adolescent, struggles to discover if he even has a father, that is, one alive, and who or what he himself shall become. In the *Iliad,* Odysseus had sometimes used the oddest of all epic formulas to describe himself : Father of Telemachus.[6] Telemachus, naturally, could have been born, at the earliest, just prior to the Trojan War, and more likely, after it had begun. Yet Odysseus uses this strange method of self-reference as though his identity were to some degree to be acquired through his son, while all other heroes in the *Iliad* base their status on the past, their pedigree, and their deeds, with Nestor a peculiarly bizarre case because of his three generations of experience. Yet Odysseus somehow receives part of his identity from the unrealized future, from the next generation. Now no one has adequately explained this odd phenomenon in the older poem, but the epithet is pregnant for the *Odyssey* itself, since the future, the new era consisting of a far more modest and settled system of political and social values, a more domestic life in general, is the whole focus of the action, and Telemachus embodies that future.[7] Telemachus, as Penelope will insist over and over again the latter half of the poem, is above all an heir, a link in historical continuity from one generation to another, and his father's absence simply endangers his inheritance. Qua father, Odysseus has been not a hero, but a delinquent father and poor custodian of family property meant to descend to his son. The tenacious insistence of the typical Mediterranean peasant on the perpetuation of property in a family stands at the back of the fierce expressions of need for Odysseus' return that he encounters in the first four books of the poem and in the last twelve. Classical scholarship, of the typical sort, has never really evaluated this evidence carefully, or even guessed at its importance.*

In beginning to read the *Odyssey* there is no way of relating to Odysseus aside from the sheer fact of his paternity. He is mainly a lost father and more vaguely a lost king. He has no presence, and his identity is felt at most as a social vacuum in the dealings of his kindred in the first four books. And the "no man" of book 9 will turn out to be a thematically true account of him. It seems hard to deny that this is a matter of careful planning by the poetic mind, for the *Odyssey* is a story of twofold, complementary, and detailed personal development on the part of son and father. First there are four books that show a

* There is something both charming and alarming about the fact that classical scholarship attained its zenith in the eighteenth and nineteenth centuries in the fogs of Oxford and the sleets of Berlin, and not in the Mediterranean basin where at the very least, simple familiarity with things like climate, social prejudices, and the growing season might have prevented so many great scholars from making colossal blunders about the life of the classical world. Martin P. Nilsson, in *Greek Popular Religion,* once made a wonderful and shrewd attempt to remind classical scholars that most of them knew nothing about the actual conditions of agriculture in Greece, and from that proceeded completely to misinterpret the myth of Demeter and Persephone. At a level of significance somewhat less crucial, but still important and annoying, one can argue that interpreters of the *Odyssey* have always neglected the importance of property and inheritance in the poem because they have no personal experience of the tenacity of this theme in the life of Mediterranean people even to this day.

society without Odysseus, then eight books showing Odysseus without a society, and then twelve books showing the slow and painful reintegration of Odysseus into his society, except that society has changed and only becomes his in stages. There is likewise a dialectical relationship in the poem between activity and stability—or perhaps stagnation. The *Odyssey* gives us a story involving a wandering person called Odysseus and a stable country called Ithaca, each seeking the other but separated by confusion as much as by space. (Similarly, in books 3 and 4, the wandering, and in other ways errant, Telemachus makes inquiries in the stable—and stagnant—societies of Pylos and Sparta, seeking old stabilities but finding only obsolete fixtures.) Odysseus and his home are separated by profound change in mentality and social realities, which the poetic intelligence behind the *Odyssey* is in no hurry to compromise or set right until the educational process has been completed, step by painful step. Odysseus can not really return home unless and until his mind has moved sufficiently from the heroic era to a new and radically changed one in which the old sort of heroism is buried and a new code of more individualized feeling and thought is in force. Ithaca in a sense is much less a geographical terminus he must reach physically than a new kind of mental landscape about which he must acquire a new consciousness if he is to see it again.

When Telemachus goes off to seek his father, he looks in the wrong places—in the apparently well-established heroic communities of Pylos and Sparta, which themselves look to the past.[8] But these are really fossil societies, relics of a dead age, useless to him and to themselves. Telemachus spends a day and a night with Nestor, who chatters on endlessly of a past even more remote than the Trojan War—which is doubly irrelevant to him and his concerns. And then he spends another day and night with Menelaus and Helen in Sparta : they are rich, comfortable, unscathed, and officially reconciled, yet they appear profoundly bored with one another, if not worse. Indeed their elaborate politeness seems barely to mask ferocious hostility. Still worse, they are *blessed*—though perhaps *condemned* is the better word— to spend an eternity with one another.[9] They are even taking drugs[10] to keep the worst effects of their ugly memories from tainting still further their useless and unending present. From them Telemachus learns the gothic tale of Agamemnon's death, the great conqueror of Troy assassinated by his wife's paramour just as he returned laden with all the glory and wealth heroic civilizations could heap upon one who carried out its imperatives and exploited its opportunities to the full. Telemachus (or at least the audience) is thus made to comprehend the two extreme types of homecoming that, in the controlling view expressed in the poem, seem possible as the heroic age comes to its apparently unlamented end : either a collapse into drugged ennui (Helen and Menelaus) or a murderous ambush (Clytemnestra and Agamemnon). There is nothing the boy could do, of course, to save his father from either fate, but the reader here is being informed that neither is satisfactory and that the homecoming of Odysseus will, and must be, different if it is to be ultimately wholesome and meaningful. (The situation found on Ithaca prior to Odysseus' return is remarkable at least in its confusion : dozens of suitors are trying to become imitation Aegisthuses, and so Odysseus will be guaranteed no dull homecoming; but at the same time we find that Penelope, the counterfoil to Clytemnestra and Helen, is somehow warding them off. so that Odysseus, unlike Agamemnon, will have the reward of wifely loyalty, but it will be a deliberately self-chosen and tested loyalty, unlike the vague repentance and drug-induced acquiescence that is all Menelaus has in Helen.)

Odysseus, on the other hand, first begins to seek his home on seagirt Ithaca in the fashion of a heroic lord, like those, including himself, who pranced, schemed, and orated before Troy : he sacks a city, with no thought that this is in any way wrong, or even ill-advised. But this will no longer do. He and his heroic consciousness must be subdued, and his thinking overhauled. Such behavior is not just morally suspect, though that question is not entirely absent from this scene, but more important it is gratuitously self-assertive, just one more case of heroic man finding a measure of his being from external and aggressive action rather than internal self-knowledge. And so heroic pillage is turned into unheroic farce: the assault is only successful because the men are away from the city, and when they return, Odysseus and his man are put to ignominious rout.* This is only the beginning of his reeducation. It will take ten years of novel experiences, alternately frightful and frustrating, to purge him of his accepted views and styles of behavior. What will he be at the end of that decade?

When Odysseus is first encountered, the decade is over—and this is important to remember—and he is marooned on the island of the seagoddess Calypso (whose name transparently means, "she who hides things"); he has been hidden from all human contact for seven full years. This has not been an entirely unpleasant exile—at least he has not lacked for sexual entertainment. But he is—finally—bored. When Hermes arrives with the decision of the gods that Calypso must let him go, he does not see Odysseus, who, the poem tells us, was sitting on the shore, weeping and staring out to sea (5.81–84). Calypso has been the last outright obstacle to the return of Odysseus to human society. Although she appears eminently reasonable in her conversation with Hermes, and even loving and gracious with Odysseus when she conveys the god's message to him later, it is clear that heretofore she has stubbornly refused to help him return home, and has in fact practised some kind of magic to keep him with her, despite his repeated wishes to leave, expressed "a thousand times before" (5.82). As he freely admits (5.215–18), her charms are quantitatively greater than those of his wife, Penelope, but the life of an immortal is no life for him. As W. S. Anderson has acutely argued, we are probably meant to

---

* Book 9.39ff. This "adventure" is a pretty sorry affair. It is indeed a "link with the Trojan war" (Whitman, note 7, p. 298), but an ironic and dismal one: Odysseus and his men manage to kill mainly animals and to steal women (9.40–41). But they have to flee the main force when the men from the city return, and their retreat is panicked and humiliating (9.47–59). So much for the heroic way of life.

see Odysseus' rejection of immortal comfort with Calypso—for to stay with her is to nullify the aging process (5.209)—as an ironic contrast with the truly dreadful fate of Menelaus, condemned as it were to an eternity of hate and boredom with Helen on the Isles of the Blessed. When Calypso suddenly offers to help him return, Odysseus immediately becomes suspicious:

> I will never embark on any raft with your anger at my back, O goddess; rather, first undertake to swear a solemn oath not to plot any harm against me.
>
> (5.177–79)

This reaction, which is probably meant to seem excessive at this point in the poem, is not something to be fully understood here but rather later, after Odysseus has recounted his adventures and made more of a case for his suspicions and scepticism. A similar vein of seemingly excessive suspicion is struck in the passage in which Odysseus, after leaving Calypso's isle on his raft, while suffering through a terrible storm, confronts the sea nymph Ino. She appears to tell him to abandon the raft, which Poseidon will surely destroy, and offers him a magic ribbon that will save him from drowning—a kind of divine lifejacket. Even here, in the face of an almost certain death, Odysseus is hostile and suspicious, and he does what an Iliadic hero never thinks of doing, he questions the direct offer of help and information from a divinity:

> Woe is me—is some divinity weaving a trick for me, to tempt me from the raft? No, I'll not obey, since I can even see land a ways off from here. . . .
>
> (5.356–59)

Although he quickly decides to change his mind when the raft starts to break up, even this momentary refusal is noteworthy, and would have been heard with amazement by Achilles' contemporaries. How had Odysseus acquired all this caution and

distrustfulness? It came as a product, first, of his general capacity
for cleverness, which is evident even in the *Iliad*. This is the
traditional picture of Odysseus. But in the *Iliad* and the tradition
it represents, Odysseus is the figure who tricks others. Partly
because the situation never arises, it never occurs to him to
suspect trickery in others—compared to his contemporaries in
the *Iliad,* he was unaware of any serious rivals as a schemer.
But here the tricker is tricked, or at least feels he might be, and
that is something new.

This newer side to Odysseus' character, however, comes not
from the general tradition but explicitly from the adventures he
has been forced to undergo in his ten years of exile, in this
poem (and by this poet), between the Cyclops and Calypso
(whose names, interestingly enough, miss by one letter each of
being perfect anagrams of one another!). The adventure of the
Cyclops has taught him a profound lesson, that the heroic code
was dead and that survival thereafter would depend on the
exercise of not just wit, but also of a grim determination and
self-discipline, especially in the very area where, as shown above,
epic heroes were so jealous and unrestrained, namely in the area
of self-identification, boasting and proclaiming their epic pedigree
and accomplishments. Odysseus is now functioning in a world
where, first, his former epic-heroic status has no meaning, and
second, *all* status is questionable, and survival depends upon
judicious manipulation or even occultation of status; and, at
rock-bottom, status includes identity. The code had failed him,
precisely at the point where its strongly felt imperatives provoked
him into a rash act—because the society he has left is known
for its rashness. Here, the rash do not live long, and the
suspicious and discreet alone survive. On the other hand,
Odysseus has learned from the adventure of the Cyclops, and
continues to do so step by step through the years, that he could
survive without the code. Having successfully gone to school for
such a long time, it just may have happened that Odysseus
has somewhat overlearned his lesson, and now thinks that the
opposite of the heroic code is the only way to live and survive,

which may help explain the mood of suspicion under consideration here, and even more the nearly psychotic suspicions and
reticences of the hero after his return home.

The next adventure begins almost beguilingly in its sim-
plicity and good cheer. Odysseus sails to the island of Aeolus,
king of the winds. After a month's hospitality Aeolus sends them
home, having packed all the adverse winds into a bag he secretly
gives Odysseus to keep. Nothing can now go wrong, and he and
his companions have sailed to within sight of Ithaca when the
crewmen begin to grumble. They wonder what is in the bag
Odysseus guards so jealously. Is it treasure, booty of some kind?
Why, they ask, has the captain not shared it, as is only right?
Then, rather suddenly, Odysseus falls asleep, they proceed to
open the bag and immediately the winds create a horrendous
storm that drives them hopelessly off course. (These unnatural
sleeps are a tantalizing problem in the poem. Why should
Odysseus sleep within sight of home? Why should he do virtually
the same thing again in book 13? I will argue in Chapter III
that sleep is almost never "natural" in the *Odyssey* and that it
serves a serious thematic and structural purpose.) After many
days lost at sea, the ship limps back to the isle of Aeolus, but
this time the god of the winds is in an entirely different frame
of mind. No longer the genial host, he is now almost the ally
of Poseidon, and sends them on with almost a duplicate of
Polyphemus' cursee :

> Crawl away from this island as fast as you can, accursed
> mortal. I have no obligation either to entertain or send off
> refreshed such a man as you are, an object of the gods'
> hatred. Begone—you have come here laden with the spite of
> the immortals!
>
> (10.72–75)

In pronouncing the sentence of the gods, as he assumes it to
be, Aeolus proclaims that Odysseus is now completely on his
own—totally and merely human and thus completely vulnerable. Aeolus thus confirms the curse of the Cyclops, which now

begins to appear more serious than Odysseus perhaps first realized. But unlike heroes in the *Iliad* who never show any resistance when cursed or otherwise brutalized by a divinity—one thinks of the story of Bellerophon, or Helen in book 3 facing Aphrodite, or of Patroclus, and then Hector, in their final moments—Odysseus does not subside into inaction. He takes the Cyclops' curse, reenforced by Aeolus, as just one more difficulty in life, just one more threat to be eluded or overcome. Whatever is in store, Odysseus is simply thrown back on his human resources to meet it. Here again is a situation that status and birth and formulaic etiquette do not cover. But neither does the curse tempt Odysseus to go limp in submission. Henceforth *problems* to be solved, neither the fixed categories of heroic society nor a baleful epic cosmology with its inescapable divine malice, are his lot in life. The curse of Aeolus is of a piece with the passage relating Odysseus' scepticism with Ino : in both cases a divine determination, whether in hostility or favor, is met with human maneuver rather than with collapse or supplication. One could very well say that passages such as these are the first representations in the history of the western mind of thinking for oneself—since there is nothing else to think with—rather than thinking controlled by preexisting patterns and superstitions; this seems to detach Odysseus still further from the heroic world of a poem like the *Iliad* where the heroes seldom if ever question the ability of divine arbitrariness to override mere human thinking.

The next adventure is the pure terror of the Laestrygones (the man-eaters), but it is disposed of briskly and one hardly remembers it, except that it begins the hero's descent into the world of the totally noncivilized. Odysseus then reaches the isle of Aeaea (roughly, "isle of moaning"), the land of Circe—witch, enchantress, and a member of a family all too famous for its experiments with the more dangerous and homicidal chemicals— she is of course Medea's aunt. Circe combines the twin threats of danger and oblivion that play a steady counterpoint in the adventures of Odysseus. She unites the motifs of Helen's drug *nepenthe* and the temptations of the Lotus Eaters, in that her drugs or charms turn men into beasts, not themselves forgetful (apparently) but likely to be forgotten. On the other hand she shares a relationship with Polyphemus, since her house, like his cave, houses beasts, to whose level men are reduced; yet again she is a sexual distraction like Calypso and also promises Odysseus a stoppage of time and the aging process, if he should consent to remain with her. Circe stands at dead center of the narrative of the adventures, and she sums up all the types of thread and delay that Odysseus encounters in his travels, with one exception, the Underworld.

It was aforementioned that the Cyclops' rock was one of the most significant milestones in the history of social thought, the answer of mere nature to the elaborate artificialities of the heroic code. The poet of the *Odyssey* has taken special pains to make us understand the reasons he had for putting the Cyclops incident into the poem. The monster is significant not simply because of his size and ferocity—that part is all folklore, which in a sense has no significance beyond the thrill of the story—but because he and his kind are said to live without social conventions, not just without the heroic code, but without *any* code at all, without the usages of sociopolitical man. The prologue to the story proper, as Odysseus himself tells it, says :

> We came to the land of the arrogant Cyclopes who acknowledge no law-custom. They, simply trusting all to the immortal gods, neither plant nor plow with their own hands; but everything grows for them unsown and unplowed—wheat, barley, vines that bear heavy clusters for wine, and the rain of Zeus makes it all grow. They have no assemblies to establish policy, nor any law-customs, but rather they live each apart on their mountain tops, in rude caves, and each one sets down the rules for children and wives, nor do they take any thought for one another.
>
> (9.106–15)

This passage excites interest even as it suggests difficulties upon comparison with the story proper that follows it. Studying the difficulties first, how does Odysseus know about the wives and children? In the actual adventure in Polyphemus' cave, there are no wives or children in evidence, and indeed a Cyclopean wife, if the giant had one, being of proportionate Cyclopean size, one assumes, could easily have prevented the blinding of her husband, or at least could have hindered Odysseus from effecting an escape from the cave afterwards. Then the remark in the lines just quoted that the Cyclopes trust the gods grates harshly on the words of Polyphemus himself at lines 275–76 : "The Cyclopes care not for Zeus who holds the aegis, nor for the other happy gods, since we are much stronger than they." (There is a material inconsistency here, since it is possible to trust in the gods in some vague way, meaning to live on nature's bounty without exertion, while still disparaging them verbally—pointing only to the unfortunate verbal inconsistency between the two adjacent passages, which, one might think, could easily have been suppressed.) Moreover, the Cyclopean diet described in the prologue has little to connect it with the cheese, milk, and flesh, both human and animal, that Polyphemus actually consumes in the story. Nor if the Cyclopes know the vine and drink wine as a matter of course, is it easy to see why the giant can be so quickly subdued by the wine of Maron Odysseus offers him, no matter how strong it is said to be, and even though it is served in large though scarcely greater-than-human proportions. But the most startling point in this bit of Cyclopean anthropology is the intimate knowledge displayed by Odysseus of the nonpolitical and even antipolitical life of the Cyclopes. Indeed, this passage is sometimes pointed to as an ancestor of the most antipolitical pastoral poetry. Yet in the tale itself as Odysseus tells it, there is nothing to suggest that he had either the interest or the opportunity to observe what political arrangements the Cyclopes do or do not have. With good reason, when faced by imminent death at the hands of a giant, one-eyed cannibal, one simply does not have the time or inclination to engage in political theory or sociological fieldwork. In addition there is some basis for the assumption that the completely antisocial existence described in the prologue is not supposed by the basic folktale that forms the body of the story. When Polyphemus has been blinded, he calls upon his fellow giants for help and they respond with at least a limited sympathy, asking the reason for his cries of pain and outrage, shouting from afar (a unique case of dramatic "business" in the history of epic, it would seem):

> . . . is some mortal stealing your sheep, or does anyone seem to be killing you by trickery or force?
>
> (9.405–6)

And it is only here that Odysseus' supposedly wily use of the false name "No man" has any purpose, and a purpose he could hardly have foreseen when he first used it. The other giants are prevented, at least verbally, from coming to Polyphemus' aid because Polyphemus answers their offers of help with the priceless line,

> Nobody kills me by a trick, nor by force.
>
> (9.408)

That "nor" is a trick of Greek grammar to which all, poet, hero, and giant are subject—perhaps the earliest literary joke in preservation, for which the rest of reading mankind remains forever in grateful debt.*

These questions are raised not to impugn the text of the prologue—though materially inconsistent with the tale itself it clearly belongs in place—but to suggest that this sociological

---

* Since the other Cyclopes have offered Polyphemus a disjunctive question—". . . by trick or by force"—Polyphemus wants to answer—indeed is required to answer by strong language conventions—in the same form, and since he is not really sure how to categorize the deed, he wants to say, "No man [conceived here as a proper name] kills me by trickery or force," but the rules of Greek grammar will not let him. Since "No man" contains the negative particle *ou,* the rule requires that all compound connectives following it in the sentence must remain in the negative mode, and so *oude,* "nor," the negative form of "or," takes its place. Had the giant simply said, "A little runt has blinded me," that would have ended the story then and there.

introduction with all its apparent and surface contradictions, and whatever its source, truly tells us of a poet's special purpose in using the story of the Cyclops. The basic story was no doubt traditional, and far older than the *Odyssey* as preserved in the version we have. In fact, since the story was probably so very popular long before any particular poet came to it, the poet no doubt faced the compositional problem of having to tell the story in something like a recognizable form, without those internal modifications that would completely harmonize it with the prologue. But the prologue is insisted on, to encase the story itself in a frame that conveys the poet's interpretation of the Cyclopean adventure to the reader, even before he reaches the story itself. He seemingly wants *this* view of the Cyclopean society, or non-society, in the record because he wants very much to make a point that could be called ideological : namely, that at the beginning of his adventures Odysseus is forced to encounter a race of beings who are perfectly opposite from the heroic world in which he had functioned heretofore. His first detailed experience, according to these lines, is with a race utterly unsympathetic with codes and usages of any kind. The Greek word translated in the previous passage, with intended clumsiness, as "law-custom," *themistes,* is a word peculiarly resistent to easy conversion into English. It means, roughly, that which is established either by law or custom and is followed by members of society more or less for its own sake. The most important usages of heroic society, such as hospitality, naming by pedigree, etc., are called *themistes* in the *Iliad.*[11] The appearance of this passage, the use of this word, clearly seem intended to register with the reader audience the fact that Odysseus is being forced by this experience with an utterly nonsocial group of creatures to seek powers and arts of survival that totally contradict his earlier experience as an epic hero. The adventure with the Cyclops thus becomes a kind of baptism into a new life, but a new life defined by reduction of Odysseus' former prerogatives and preconceptions, to a bare minimum and lowest common denominator. This is most effectively summed up by his adoption of the name "No man," the ultimate form of resignation from heroic society. The fact that the prologue of the Cyclops story fails in matters of detail to correspond to the subsequent narrative only argues how insistent the poet was in obtaining this particular understanding of the adventure before his audience.

A return to Circe is necessary—but only for a moment. Circe sends Odysseus to the Underworld to interview Teirisias, who alone of the dead retains intelligence and tells Odysseus how to return home. D. L. Page has written many pages of dry comedy on this passage, proving to his own satisfaction that not only is it the product of multiple authorship, but has been subject to editing by lunatics.[12] This is because, as it turns out, Teirisias has his facts all wrong and gives Odysseus only useless information; and then when Odysseus returns to Aeaea and Circe one finds that Circe has known all along how he is to return home and sets about sending him there. Thus, it is clear, the Circe story has been divided and the Underworld story, from a different source, has been inserted between the halves. Yet this by itself does not prove that one man did not split the Circe story to insert an epic passage of a different origin in the space thus created; nor, perhaps more important, does it prove that the Hades visit, book 11, has no particular purpose in the overall design of the poem, however many designers there may be. (For one thing, there just may be arguments going to suggest that the trip to the Underworld may have been an hallucination, induced by drugs, and not real at all, a point taken up in the Appendix.) In any case, supposing that a poet wanted Odysseus to go to Hades, for reasons of his own, what would it take to motivate the hero to go? Obviously, directions or something else needed to help him reach home! The fact that he does not get those directions where he is told to get them, but only later, back where he was told to undertake the journey in the first place, will simply call attention, and give greater emphasis to, what he does get. It will not do to scorn book 11 as a weird patchwork, as Page does. Finding evidence of four joints in the fabric does not relieve us of the task of investigating the fabric's purpose. The expedition to interview Teirisias, which proves fruitless for that purpose, is also an opportunity for the poet to make Odysseus submit, first, to a review of ancient heroines whose sexual histories, one way and another, conspire to make him anxious about Penelope. (His mother's odd story does little to help out here. According to Anticleia, Penelope is weeping in his house, Telemachus is a magistrate, "feasting and being feasted," and Laertes is poor as a churchmouse and forced to sleep among the slaves. The first statement is true but maddeningly inexact, the second false, and the third inscrutible, for when we meet Laertes at the end of the poem he is obviously in retirement, out working in his orchards, but that he is destitute would be hard to prove—more likely would be the average reader's guess that he is simply going senile.) Of the heroines, Odysseus observes, Tyro was seduced by Poseidon, Antiope and Alcmene by Zeus—in the latter case with Zeus adopting the true husband's figure, as a disguise, an obvious forward reference to Odysseus' ambiguous feelings when Penelope sets the Contest of the Bow: she will marry whoever strings the bow, she says, that is, either Odysseus or anyone sufficiently like him to perform the task. Then there are Epicaste (Jocasta), who lived incestuously with her son; Phaedra, who had incestuous feelings towards her stepson; and her sister Ariadne, who was abandoned on the island of Naxos by Theseus for some unnamed sexual transgression. These are then followed by Clymene and Eriphyla, who betrayed and ambushed their husbands—which is precisely the fate that Odysseus anxiously is beginning to feel could attend his own homecoming. After a formal break in the narration in which King Alcinous commends his storytelling ability, Odysseus resumes his tale: he confronted a second group of shades, the souls of his dead heroic comrades, whose words combine to do two things—they create still more anxiety in him, and they indicate that the heroic world and its code is just as dead as they are. First, Agamemnon tells the story of his own betrayal and murder by Clytemnestra and her lover Aegisthus, the same story that Telemachus learned from Menelaus in book 4, and the audience learned of from the Council of Zeus in book 1. As one reads on, of course, the responsibility of Aegisthus, upon which Zeus had insisted, shrinks at each retelling by human informants, and by the time one reaches Agamemnon's ghost and its version of the tale (is a ghost human? a proper question here, one should think), both Clytemnestra and woman's untrustworthiness in general have become the chief concern. Naturally, each succeeding version of the tale ripens the anxieties of the audience for Odysseus' ultimate fate, and each succeeds in making them at least momentarily receptive to Odysseus' deep distrust of his wife—until they recall that he had heard only Agamemnon's version, and not those of Zeus and Menelaus.

Agamemnon's justifiable malice against his destroyers somehow slides over the line dividing what readers must think is appropriate, however, and into the area of a rather sickening sadism :

> Learn from this never to be easy with a woman, not even you, nor tell them all you know, but say this, while keeping that a secret. But of course, Odysseus, your death will never come from a wife's hands! Penelope daughter of Icarius is too shrewd and knows policy too well for that.
>
> (11.441–46)

These words hardly give Odysseus much assurance, and are strangely motivated in the dramatic sense. In his tale of treason Agamemnon does not indicate that anything he told or did not tell Clytemnestra had anything to do with his own murder. Again, this looks suspiciously like a forward reference, prophetic of Odysseus on his return, guarding his every word and glance, especially with Penelope. It heralds the endless prevarications with which Odysseus repels her curiosity when he finally meets her in his disguises as a shipwrecked vagabond. And it supplies at least a part of their motivation : Penelope is wise, even clever, Agamemnon insinuates, and whatever she does or seems to be doing just conceivably might look as though she is only playing angles and percentages against even her husband. Moreover, the word translated as *policy* above could also have an obscene sense, for the Greek word *medea* sometimes means, in the circumspect language of the Lexicon, *virilia*, the male organs: is Agamemnon hinting with a smirk that Penelope has an eye for masculinity? Possibly, for—in general—Agamemnon's ghost delights in vulgar speech.[13] If this were not enough to unhinge Odysseus, the ghost of Achilles arrives to dismantle the other mainstay of his former self-confidence, his belief in the reality and meaning of the heroic career. This scene is quite clearly set up by the poet to accomplish an act of demolition. When he sees Achilles' ghost, among all the things he might have said, Odysseus gauchely chooses to congratulate Achilles for his heroic career during life, with some remarkably ill-chosen words: Achilles was the most blessed of men who came before or will follow after him; when he was alive Odysseus and all the Argives honored him as the equal of a god; even in Hades he is obviously a great power among the dead: (and finally, pure bathos) therefore Achilles should not be angry at having died (11.483–86). In its way this speech is as preposterous and unfeeling as Agamemnon's to him a moment before, but Achilles at least has the "freedom of speech" that death confers, and shouts bitterly,

> Worthy Odysseus, do not praise death to me. For I would rather be working as the hired man of a tenant farmer on earth—a man who had nothing at all—than to rule over the strengthless dead.
>
> (11.488–91)

With these lines a complete transformation of values takes place. Achilles, the quintessential hero of the *Iliad,* of the whole epic tradition, is changed in the *Odyssey* into a remorseful, bitter ghost who in four climactic lines turns the whole heroic image and premise over into the dust. Yet he is also a prophet—and a true one, unlike the caddish Agamemnon—for indeed Odysseus will seem to serve for a time as the hired man of Eumaeus, the pig-keeping slave who first shelters him when he returns to Ithaca, in order to preserve life, that which Achilles now declares the supreme good, no matter what the conditions required for keeping it. This is a condition we can imagine no Homeric hero tolerating, but, as Achilles says, Odysseus will have life, and that is the important thing! (It is worth noting that this speech takes much the same line as that other great antiheroic manifesto, Falstaff's speech about honor: What is honor? A word. What is a word but air? Who has it? He "who died a'Wednesday . . . for it will not live with the living." The point in both cases being that death makes a hero, a man honored for his dying bravery. and thus in a sense there are no heroes; there only have been heroes! To continue living is to fail of absolute honor and heroism, and is thus to be no better than anyone else, forced to compromise and maneuver.)

Although Odysseus has been undergoing a steady process of recession from the heroic code and its ambitions through his adventures, if we had to mark the book and line where he irrevocably opts for life over death, where he is finally forced to do so regardless of lingering preferences for the past and its certitudes, for survival and self-control over fatal self-assertion of status, for maneuver over the code, this is the place. This is made doubly clear by the fact that Odysseus rejects immortality with Calypso in book 5 only after he has toured the Underworld and heard Achilles' words in book 11 (simply giving the book numbers symbolizes the convolutions of time involved at the poet's command), and only after one has learned from book 4, in the Helen–Menelaus story, that immortality conferred on the once-mortal is likely to be hateful and boring rather than pleasant. He has learned a profound lesson: to choose life is to reject both the heroic case for glorious death as well as even a god's reward of, or arguments for, a redundant immortality, that does not fit the human species. What Achilles thought of the matter is not entirely clear, but Odysseus certainly does not understand his ghost to be saying that one can live forever if one rejects heroic grandeur—only that one should survive as long as possible. Either to long for immortality or to court death (with honor) are both attempts to dishonor life and denature it.

But to choose life over both immortality as well as a fatalistic love of glory is only half the tale. To be fully human requires more than just staying alive as long as one can; Odysseus has learned only half his lesson. In a way it is on Scheria, the isle of the fabled Phaecians, that Odysseus faces his most serious trials, save those of Ithaca itself. Having lost his last crewmen on the island of Thrinacia because they ate the cattle of Helios—and thus losing the last vestige of heroic office, namely command over others—Odysseus had come to Calypso and had spent seven years of total anonymity with her. Finally released, as seen, he battles one last storm and is washed ashore on Scheria. He is finally near home; the people of Scheria, unlike all his other hosts, are a real human society (or are they? C. R. Beye has pointed out that Scheria is just as fanciful and weird an adventure as Ogygia, Aeaea, or the unnamed isle of the Cyclopes.[14] The Phaeacians may not be monsters or witches, but they are odd, and in some quaint ways ahistorical. They have never left the now-dead heroic age, though they are apart from it, as a kind of exempt society.) Here the challenge is, for once, not physical but moral. To survive at all, in his adventures from the Cyclops to Calypso, Odysseus had to develop a preternatural skepticism and caution. But 'on Scheria, one stop from home, caution itself poses a different kind of threat. Part of humanity, certainly the best part, is spontaneity, acting out of the fullness of one's nature and excellence rather than from plan or ideology. One may view Scheria as largely a therapeutic way-station to allow Odysseus to begin reacquiring the skills of social plausibility before he reenters the actual world of Ithaca, though it is only a weak and painful beginning. But this of course is not what his stay on Scheria actually accomplishes for him, whatever it may do to increase the tension and enrich the realism, the moral realism, of the story. No, Odysseus cannot make very comfortable use of the hospitality of Scheria because, along with heroic assumptions, he has effectively purged all human spontaneity from his soul and his system in his ten years of exile. And on Scheria the unnatural effects of this purgation begin to appear, and to become the dominant facts about his temperament, eclipsing the cleverness and resourcefulness of the earlier books.

The hero's caution does of course spring from real—or mostly real—events, and it is perfectly understandable. The adventure of the Cyclops first taught him the value of caution, and self-effacement, and every day and every new encounter rehearsed that lesson for him. If the adventures are traced backwards, one notices that Odysseus is more cautious with Calypso than with Circe, more cautious with Circe than with the Cyclops. (And, as we shall see, he is most cautious of all with Penelope.) At some point, caution has ceased to be merely a defensive device and has become an all-pervasive obsession. On Scheria it is revealed as a grotesque mask of the man underneath, and threatens to become a moral threat to his homecoming, when physical threats shall be largely behind him. One who has learned too well to commune solely and totally with himself alone, even if he should transcend the limits of the heroic code by doing so, will ultimately be too isolated to be a member of society once again.

The events on Scheria do little or nothing to dispel this caution, and many of them seem to be designed by the poet primarily to make us realize how far Odysseus has gone in this direction. Even in the toy society of the Phaeacians, Odysseus finds it nearly impossible for him to reconstitute the normal functioning bonds a man has with his, or any, society of fellow men. He is morally and socially arthritic, if not quite paralytic. The land of the Phaeacians is introduced not simply to allow Odysseus to tell his story to strangers—which is one purpose, but a purpose required only by the apparently deliberate, and larger, purpose of turning the plot upside down, so that Odysseus can tell his adventures long after they have happened; while one can therefore observe the moral change they have effected in him, even if he cannot, and before one has seen the specific reasons that go toward explaining it, namely the course of the adventures themselves. The episode on Phaeacia, in a most important sense, allows the poet to tell what has happened to Odysseus' character, within and alongside the narrative in which he permits Odysseus the character to tell the literal details of his story.

After waking up on the beach in a clump of wild olive, Odysseus encounters the princess Nausicaa, who has been directing her maids at washing the household linen, and participating in an unscheduled and noisy game of ball. A badly aimed ball actually wakens Odysseus, and the two meet. They bandy words at great length, and eventually fall to making elaborate plans for getting Odysseus into the city and into the king's audience chamber, where, as a suppliant on the hearth, he has the virtual right to demand assistance in getting home. Odysseus, it need hardly be said, has not come near identifying himself to Nausicaa, and has fabricated a story about his identity and origins to win her sympathy. The plans they make seem to presuppose that this enterprise is fraught with great risks and awful uncertainty, yet, in the event, there is no danger of risk that one can perceive at all. Their plan for Odysseus to rush to the hearth and demand sanctuary—not to mention the goddess Athena's utterly unnecessary intervention into the plot—presupposes that King Alcinous is generally a man to be feared for some notorious hostility to strangers—a characteristic of which not one more word is heard as the actual events unfold! Why then this intense overture of strategem and suspicion to what is now at most a minor complication in Odysseus' return home? The reason, I think, is that this is simply the way Odysseus' mind works at this moment. (One must remember that he does not tell this part of the story—the poet does; and I suspect that Athena's behavior here is aimed mainly at making his behavior credible to Nausicaa, who is obviously impressed with strategems and dark purposes, a scheming female, again an ambiguous forward reference to Penelope. Athena, here, is help-less to change Odysseus, and she goes along with the schemes more or less on the theory that it is better to do something than nothing.) Why, again, is Nausicaa portrayed as so full of worldly wisdom and suspicion at her tender age? (No realism here : this is simply the only kind of person Odysseus is equipped to deal with at the moment. Had she been a silly young thing Odysseus would no doubt simply have jumped back into the sea.) Some critics, and many students, perhaps overly alert to the hero's sexual capacities, have seen this episode as a prelude to a love affair that never quite comes off. I think not. Odysseus has had any number of love affairs by now, and they have come more easily than he could have imagined. To him, a wife, properly understood, is an entirely different sort of being from a casual amour. A wife is an ally in defending property, maintaining her husband's good name, and shrewdly managing a household —romantic attractions are not to the point. Odysseus' remark that Nausicaa would make a fine wife (book 6.158–59) probably has more to do with her boldness in meeting him, and the implied bravery and shrewdness within her character, than with her physical desirability : it simply confirms his present frame of mind and his complex of hopes and fears about his wife. (And in any case, for Odysseus sexual attraction has little to do with wives—he who has lain with goddesses. A wife, on the other hand, is a political and social bulwark—or flaw—in the family edifice, a defender or betrayer of her husband's position and property and therefore of his life; she is not thought of, pri-marily, as an object of sexual lust. Agamemnon's ghost, if not other considerations, had made that point to Odysseus.) As we shall see, Penelope will fail to confirm her husband's fears and expectations in two ways : she will have been proven totally faithful and tenacious about the family fortunes and honor, insofar as she was able, but she will also be seen as cautious only to a point, and dangerously spontaneous and impolitic to a fault—in declaring the Contest of the Bow—when that point is passed, and much too ready to take risks that the chastened Odysseus has learned to avoid, at the cost of hard experience. There he will find real grounds for disappointment in her, if not real fear of disaster. (Penelope's weakness, her possession of a natural and believable breaking point, despite her strengths, will mark her as fully human, which her husband is not, and does not want to be, until she finally tricks him the way he has tricked others, and all too successfully for his own moral vitality.)

Odysseus fails to identify himself (again!) upon first reaching the Phaeacian court, and he is allowed to get away with it. Then, when the bard Demodocus sings of the Trojan adventure and mentions his own name prominently, he covers his face and weeps (book 8.83–86). We are now far indeed from the epic hero who shouted his identity across the water to Polyphemus. In fact this scene sketches with terrible clarity just what the poem, ultimately, is all about. It says that the progress of an epic hero, from one age and one set of standards with which he felt in complete harmony, to another age and its standards that have seen the last of such heroes, is hardly a pleasant jaunt through the Greek isles, nor even a stirring series of doughty adventures, but a fearful exercise that rends the soul more than the body, because it torments the former hero with the final conundrum about his identity. It is one thing to hear a bard telling the good old stories, as Demodocus does here, if one accepts them as old and quite thoroughly past and beyond recovery; it is quite another thing to be an old story, a leftover from another age, and to hear what amounts to one's own obituary. This scene summarzies the crisis in the hero's personality and states precisely what his problem is: to reconstruct a new personality that will permit him to function in a new sort of world. He no longer *is* the Odysseus of epic adventure, because, among other reasons, that Odysseus has been frozen into epic poetry remorselessly stamped as ancient, alien and beyond reach; and when he hears his career thus recounted, he can no longer react as though it were properly his at all—he is at most the heir, not the author, of the deeds, a saddened relict of what is almost another man's life. The progress of social events on Scheria makes all this even more terribly clear. Having failed to identify himself, as an epic hero would, Odysseus then goes on to illustrate just how far he has traveled from the heroic era and its usages by systematically misplaying or ignoring social cues signaled to him by Phaeacian society, which is not exactly heroic itself but plays at living in an archaic past by imitating at least the minor social protocols of that past. This society does not fight epic battles or engage in other forms of high heroic bravery, but it dearly loves athletic games, solemn feasts, and the recitations of the great heroic feats of others by its court bard. Odysseus fails to take the expected pleasure his hosts anticipate he would in first one form of recollected epic behavior, namely listening to the recitation of military exploits even though they are his own. Soon thereafter he tries to avoid the opportunity for athletic competition, refusing a challenge by Laodamas, the king's son, to partake in games of strength and skill that have been inaugurated in his honor! And worse, he argues that his sorrowful experiences and the preoccupied state of his thoughts would not let him concentrate on anything so trivial as sports (8.153–54). Ultimately, taunted more openly by another cadet of the Phaeacian nobility, he in fact agrees to compete and without bothering to strip flings the discus for a record and first prize, over which he entirely neglects to gloat. It is clear that he has so acted to still all the talk his refusal created and to teach his tormentor a lesson. It means nothing to him, as he points out: he has suffered through real contests in which the prize was life, and death the penalty for failure (8.179ff.), and he is as good at this sort of thing as any man living, even though—a nice qualification from one who has undergone the transformation he has faced—he is no match for the men of old (8.221ff.), like Heracles or Eurytus. The whole scene is remarkable: much of the heroic view of life as unrestrained action and ruthless competition for honors and glory in the public eye now toppled in the dust of the athletic field, first scorned, and the second time indulged in with distaste and irony. Odysseus' first refusal of the challenge, his contempt for sports, the implication that something occupying his mind is more significant than the outward, objective honor one wrests from others by winning contests, in any sort of competition, no matter how tedious or unnecessary, reminds us by contrast of the frantic and quite dishonest competition among some of the Greek heroes of the *Iliad* for prizes at the funeral games for Patroclus.[15] The quarrel between Idomeneus and Ajax, for instance, over alleged cheating in a chariot race, is very little lower in tone or decibels than the far more serious quarrel between Achilles and Agamemnon twenty-two books earlier, which, one could say, led to the events that made this ritual of games necessary. Yet another example of how he *Odyssey* abandons one after another of the picked and chosen strong points of the heroic landscape, and in abandoning it, stops to ridicule it with not just verbal irony proceeding from the main character Odysseus himself, but with narartive irony : Odysseus who had seen the grandest of the epic grandees fight like fishwives over evanescent prizes at Troy, now finds it barely tolerable to participate in the same sort of contest here in backwater community where he is clearly the best competitor, and uses his victory to lecture his challengers about the vanity of such contests and their essential frivolity compared with real contests and conflicts that threaten a man's life.

Feasting is another important social ritual in heroic society, and of course even Odysseus must eat, but one can not help noticing how he now approaches the matter, when responding to the king's proclamation of a feast to honor him :

There is nothing comparable, for doglike manners, to the belly; it constantly bids us remember it and works at troubling even the man who is sorrowful to the heart. Thus, I. who have a full share of grief in my heart, even I am under

orders to eat and drink, and I am made to forget my troubles
while I endeavor to satisfy my belly.

(7.216–21)

This is in fact Odysseus' first direct speech to King Alcinous.
He does not seem to regard feasting as any kind of high
ceremony, but simply a vulgar and demanding necessity, with
nothing romantic or very pleasant about it—indeed the belly
will not even let a sorrowful man concentrate on his sorrows.
We are reminded by contrast of Achilles' refusal in the *Iliad*
to take food when he is in a rage to avenge the death of his
friend Patroclus, and Odysseus' several speeches at that point
in praise of breakfast.[16] And finally—to recur to the opening
question of this chapter and to revive the point made there—as
Odysseus begins to tell his own story to his hosts, he only pro-
nounces his own name, Odysseus son of Laertes, after the
transition to book 9 and thus only within the framework of the
Polyphemus story in which he both denied his own identity and,
for the last time in the tale, used his own name! Here Odysseus
becomes his own bard, but unlike Demodocus, who told a story
about his cleverness and his epic successes, at which he remained
silent, he names himself only here, at the beginning of a tale
largely given to recounting his failures, fears, and frustrations,
which is what the adventures really come to when read carefully.
    The final explanation of Odysseus' present caution on
Scheria, his seeming revulsion from the entertainments of the
old heroic life, his preoccupation with things far beyond the
commonly known world, his persistent sadness and his tenacious
suspicions, is perhaps best to be found in the fact that for ten
years with the exception of his crew, who are merely a narrative
necessity and convenience, Odysseus has met only subhuman,
superhuman, and, *sit venia verbo,* posthuman beings, that is,
monsters, divinities, and the dead. Nor are the Phaeacians quite
human, either. They look human enough, but they do not seem
to die, and they stand outside history, living in a kind of
meaningless past; "Scheria . . . is just as fabulous and marginal

as the various stations in the travel stories. Homer reminds us
that the Phaeacians had once been the neighbors of the Cyclopes
and that now in Scheria they were 'far from mankind who must
work to exist.' "[17] The purgation of heroic values in Odysseus
required by the design of the poem or poet in turn has required
just this sort of alienation from human contact, but the moral
costs to the hero are very high, and the most painful part of
his return will be the lengths to which the tale must take him
in reeducating him to view human beings as merely human,
neither epic heroes like the Achilles or the Odysseus of yore, nor
superhuman beings of infinite cleverness and guile, like the multi-
tude of monsters, godlings, shades, and goddesses that have filled
his days for a decade. Real human beings, like Penelope, have
a limit in their ability to engage in schemes and stratagems. The
Odysseus one comes to know at the end of this decade of exile
has effectively forgotten this, under the stress of his own experience. There have been no human limits to his capacity for
suspicion and caution and scheming, simply because there have
been none to the agencies threatening him, but the process that
finally stripped him of heroic bravado also buried his humanity,
and exhuming it will be the task of the remaining books of
the *Odyssey*.

The tedium of Scheria, as indicated, is more useful to the
poet than to his hero. First, it portrays the hero's social
paralysis, his discomfort with traditional hospitality and entertainments that once were the equal of life itself to him and
every other hero. But there is one more important device to
consider, the story told by the poet Demodocus of Ares and
Aphrodite and their singularly unfortunate adultery (8.266 ff.).
The point the story makes, told in this place, is, if any, to strike
a contrast between the giddy and inconsequential immoralities
of the Homeric gods, and the serious consequences of such
behavior in the new, human world of our poem, under new
laws that apply, at least by inference, even to the gods, if one
can believe the protestations of Zeus in book 1. Whether this
version of divine dalliance is a fairly typical example of peasant

moralizing against aristocratic standards of behavior, is not a question that can take up our time here, but it is at least clear that the outcome of the tale, the capture of Ares and Aphrodite *in flagrante delictu,* by means of a trick, and their acute embarrassment over it, is at least a case that the poet's audience was meant to view as one of condign punishment meted out to those who violate marriage oaths and the sanctity of the family, though the culprits are in this case divine and can suffer no greater hurt than the embarrassment itself. (One may compare this result with the results of Aegisthus' adultery, as announced by Zeus in book 1, to see how much more grievous are the results among men.) The story also raises, albeit in the comic mode, the specter of the aggrieved husband's revenge, and this aspect of it would not be missed by Odysseus as he listens. It suggests to him that if Penelope shall have proved unfaithful, he will have to seek his vengeance, not as an epic hero might, bursting into the house armed to teeth and shouting war cries, but as the crippled, repulsive Hephaestus does, through stealth and trickery even while submitting to the jeers and laughter of others (the other gods always jeer and hoot at Hephaestus, just as Odysseus is jeered at by the suitors, and even some of his own slaves). Hephaestus is a prefiguring of Odysseus himself diguised as a contemptible beggar on Ithaca, mocked in his own home while he plots, or at least dreams of, a complex revenge. And Hephaestus' mesh, so fine that it can not be seen, is a prefiguring of the elaborate plotting and indirection the disguised hero employs in his seemingly endless maneuvers with (or against?) his wife. So the story works on his mind. There is just one trouble with it : Penelope is faithful and a plot in the style of Hephaestus will be, as it turns out, mostly waste motion. There is nothing he has to fear from Penelope, and much of Odysseus' caution will seem plainly perverse. To be sure, some caution will be necessary with the suitors, since they are cutthroats (they plot to ambush Telemachus, for instance). But by and large Odysseus' problem on Ithaca will not be to punish an adulterous wife but to rescue her, first from the suitors, and then from her nightmares and despondency. But the device necessary for this task is not going to be subtlety or double-meaning craft—just the opposite. What Penelope will need most is assurance that she can now relax her ten-years' vigil, that she can give herself over to emotion and depend for a time on someone else. And for this to happen, Odysseus must finally identify himself to her. Finding the courage for that act, given the condition his mind is now in, will be the most difficult of all the trials he has faced, not so much for his genius, but for his character.

Notes

1. W. J. Woodhouse, *Composition of Homer's Odyssey* (Oxford: Clarendon Press, 1930), pp. 216–17.

2. *See* Rhys Carpenter, *Folk Tale, Fiction and Saga in the Homeric Epics* (Berkeley and Los Angeles: University of California Press, 1946), chs. 1, 7; *See also* D. L. Page, *The Homeric Odyssey* (Oxford: Oxford University Press, 1955), ch. 1; and J. E. Frazer, ed. and tr., *Apollodorus* (London: William Heineman, 1931, The Loeb Classical Library, Appendix 13. Frazer has assembled thirty-six folktales parallel to the Cyclops adventure. Of that number, nine tales have the hero mocking the giant (or giantess, tale 11) after his escape, but in only one of these does the hero use his name to complete the insult (tale 33). On the other hand, in none of these is there any play on a name comparable with Odysseus' use of "No man." There is name-play in only two other tales of Frazer's collection, neither associated with a challenge or boast: tale 10 uses "myself" to play a trick on the Devil and get him punished unintentionally and its plotting value is different, springing from the "devil-is-an-ass" theme of the morality play; and tale 12 uses "nobody" but the point is not carried further than a mild joke with no plot consequences. Oskar Hackman, *Die Polyphemsage in der Volküberlieferung* (Helsingfors: see Biblio p. 124 "Hackman" 1904), p. 179, rejects all tales that combine the "No man" episode with an escape episode as having no independent testimonial value for an *Urmotif* earlier than the *Odyssey* itself, considering them as "contaminated" by the presence and knowledge of the *Odyssey* itself; he recognizes, pp. 107–33, that there are many tales recording name-play (he has found forty-nine), but only one has any connection with a blinded giant, sheep, etc., and this is a clear case of contamination (p. 190).

3. *See* C. R. Beye, *The Iliad, the Odyssey and the Epic Tradition* (New York: Doubleday, 1966), pp. 180–81.

4. *See* Wiglaf's funeral oration over Beowulf: "Now there shall cease for your race the receiving of treasure and the giving of swords, all enjoyment of pleasant homes, comfort. Each man of your kindred must go deprived of his land-right when nobles from afar learn of your fright, your inglorious deed" (sec. 39); "Now may the people expect a time of war, when the

king's fall becomes well-known . . ." (sec. 40). Tr. E. T. Donaldson (New York: W. W. Norton Co. 1966).

5. *Iliad* 7.123pff. Nestor is atempting to meddle in the proposed duel between Menelaus and Hector, who is substituting for the vanished Paris; Agamemnon wisely—for once—realizes that Menelaus is no match for Hector and begs him not to risk his life; Nestor, foolishly—as usual—insists that the duel proceed and paints a falsely glorious picture of what the duel will do for Menelaus' glory—then he wanders off the track: "Alas, a great woe had come to Achaea, and the great horse-tamer Peleus would groan aloud, the great councilor and lord of the Myrmidons . . . he who once upon a time questioned me closely in his home—and it gave him great pleasure—to learn the family and descent of each of the Argive leaders. . . ."

6. For example, *Iliad* 2.26: "May I not be called father of Telemachus. . . ." This appears to be a kind of oath, a self-imposed conditional curse—going without progeny—unless something is accomplished.

7. *See* Cedric Whitman, *Homer and the Epic Tradition* (Cambridge: Harvard University Press 1958), p. 309: "The old Achaean world reappears in Pylos and Sparta, *in order to acquaint Telemachus with his heritage.* One hears high tales of it from Demodocus, but the people of whom he sings are not of it, except for Odysseus himself." The italics are mine: to me, Whitman seems correct in sensing that the scenes at Pylos and Sparta are meant to picture a time now past, but I suggest that their purpose is hardly "to acquaint Telemachus with his heritage," especially since, as we shall see, that heritage is so sterile, malevolent and dangerous. The purpose is rather to warn him of the extremely serious mistake he would be making if he were to assume that the old values and standards, by which his father also once lived, are any longer valid, or offer any hope of protecting his father and helping him reclaim his home. Telemachus—or at least the reader—is being informed that if Odysseus has not moved beyond these standards he is worse than dead, he is archaic and useless as an example, even to his own son.

8. Whitman, *ibid.*

9. The elaborate sickness of the relationship between Helen and Menelaus at Sparta is developed with very great care by W. S. Anderson, "Calypso and Elysium," pp. 73–86 in C. H. Taylor, ed., *Essays on the Odyssey* (Bloomington, Ind.: Indiana University Press, 1963). Anderson's most important point is that the neurotic and drugged immortality of Helen and Menelaus is a suggestive counterfoil to Odysseus' eventual *refusal* of a not-so-different sort of immortality with Calypso.

10. Anderson, *ibid.* On the use of drugs in the poem overall, *see* the appendix.

11. See *Iliad* 1.238 and 11.779, for example.

12. Page (note 1 above), chapter 2. Though Page's many interests do not seem to include a concern for the meaning of a work of literature, he still is always worth reading for his rambunctious style and sometimes screamingly funny delivery. Chapter 2 of *The Homeric Odyssey* rivals some

of Mark Twain's better pages on medieval culture—Page's distance from his subject is approximately the same, as well.

13. Clytemnestra is a "dogface" (11.424); nothing is more "accursed and doglike" than a woman (11.427); other coarse animal similes punctuate his speech.

14. *See* Beye (note 3 above), pp. 159–160.

15. *See Iliad* 23.

16. This topic is the subject of one of funnier scenes in the *Iliad*—in book 19.155 ff. there is a mock "debate" between Odysseus and Achilles over the propriety of Achilles' eating before he goes out to requite the death of Patroclus by doing battle with Hector. Achilles, naturally, feels no hunger at a time like this; Odysseus can seemingly not get off the subject of food. For more laughs still, see again D. L. Page, *History and the Homeric Iliad* (Berkeley and Los Angeles: University of California Press 1963), p. 314.

17. *See* Beye (note 3 above), pp. 194–95.

2

The Disguised Guest

ODYSSEUS AND ITHACA, EACH SEEKING THE OTHER, ARE
separated not just by space but by mental confusion, on both
sides. Odysseus' confusion is that in all his years outside the real
world of human beings he has eventually shed his identification
with the code of the epic hero, which is obviously obsolete and
flawed—if one can take Achilles' ghost as an expert on the
subject. But this change was accomplished by depriving Odysseus
of all human contact, so that he now is afflicted by a marked
inability to function among men, of every and any class and
kind. This was clear in his behavior at the Phaeacian court, and
it becomes marked and critical upon his return to Ithaca. Living
again even in a quasi-human society like Scheria is an art that
Odysseus has forgotten along with his heroic heraldry, and
desperately needs to relearn. Unfortunately he does not realize
his own needs. All those years of facing danger from nonhuman
sources and of overcoming despair in his loneliness have led him
to renounce heroic show and self-proclamation for the opposite
arts, the inward and inscrutable arts of survival at almost any
cost. These arts save his mere existence, of course, but conceal-
ment and stealth do not make very healthy constant companions,
and in his case they have finally become not simply means of
survival, but ends in themselves. Though meant to help him find
his way back to his former life, they become instead the substance
of his life now! When he returns to Ithaca it is as though to one
more foreign island conceivably ruled by one more untrustworthy

power who intends evil for him. He sees Ithaca as embodying all the real or imagined threats of all the other islands on his itinerary : that of the Cyclops with its physical terror; the isle of Aeolus with disappointment, frustration, and despair arising from the wind god's curse; Circe's Aeaea with its enchantments; Thrynacia with its temptations to self-destruction; Calypso's Ogygia with its seduction and boredom; and finally, Scheria with its museumlike unreality, its now appalling replay of dead heroic customs, plus the disconcerting apparent prophecy in the Ares–Aphrodite tale sung by Demodocus. But actually the danger on Ithaca stems from another source entirely, the threat of the very lesson he has massively overlearned, that to survive in extra-ordinary circumstances one must be intensely wary. But not all circumstances are extraordinary, and eventually to live a fully human life one must be able to relax and put one's trust in the company of other men, assuming, for instance, that on most occasions ordinary men speak and act as they really intend. Coming home then will not be the simple act Odysseus had thought. It is he himself who complicates the matter. The real struggle, the most intense adventure, is to come : the struggle with himself to tear away the guise of cunning otherness, of alien strangerhood, of programmatic deceit with others, and to realize in his innards that he really is home, that this is his place. To realize that he can no longer play the empty envelope, the No Man capable of being filled with any arbitrary personal history that might fit the current scheme; that he is no longer in the position of the uncommitted refugee, sharply calculating how to slip away from danger on the next outgoing tide. On Ithaca his problem will be not to find the quickest exit, but to acquiesce in the fact that there are no exits from one's own place, and that there are no good grounds for the use of disguises and false tales with one's own people, even if the suitors remain to be beguiled a bit further. Here the challenge will be to admit his identity courageously, and Odysseus nearly fails the most import-ant challenge of his whole life. (This view of the meaning of the last half of the poem is at variance with the most common understanding of it, and even seems to contradict such things as Athena's willingness to help Odysseus remain in disguise. Such a broad reinterpretation cannot be dealt with in a few footnotes, and I ask the reader to read the whole course of my arguments in this chapter and the next as my justification for these bold statements.)

The *Odyssey* could be viewed as little more than an endlessly complex study of the possible ramifications of the guest–host relationship, where the guest is nearly always in some form of disguise. This theme is announced, as it were in a minor key, at the opening of the poem, specifically book 1.105ff., where the goddess Athena appears to Telemachus in the guise of Mentes, an old family friend. Nothing so odd, it would at first seem, about this: the gods do that sort of thing all the time, to help, hurt, or spy on men. In fact, at one point a suitor speculates whether the disguised Odysseus might not actually be a god sent to observe their behavior.[1] But the Athena–Mentes scene is only the beginning of a great procession of disguised guests. Even before the Wanderings proper, the guest–host relationship has been turned in every direction, so that every facet is struck by the light, and each reflects some new social and literary insight.

Let us consider only the following cases. Either in direct narrative or flashback one has: Telemachus as a guest of Nestor at Pylos, not literally in disguise but not quickly identified and inhibited by youthful reticence from truly functioning in the fossil society of Pylos. In Sparta Telemachus hears Helen tell the tale of Odysseus' secret mission into Troy—and a spy is a special sort of disguised guest—and how she protected him. (The story is told, no doubt, not for the boy's benefit, but to make the point in Menelaus' hearing that she was always really loyal to the Greek cause,[2] though it seems doubtful he believes her.) Next, Menelaus tells his tale recalling another event involving Odysseus, namely that of the Trojan horse, relating with feeling how Odysseus stopped the mouth of one of the Greeks who was severely tempted to cry out when Helen prowled around the horse cleverly imitating the voices of the men's wives. (This, of course, is meant mainly to rebut Helen's implied claim of loyalty, since her purpose could only serve the Trojan cause.[3]) The Greeks in the horse, surely, were another sort of disguised guest. Moreover they were guests disguised with a beast-guise—this to become a major sub-category of the overall theme of disguises. The subtheme is repeated in Menelaus' tale of how he captured the wily seagod Proteus on his own difficult voyage home. To do so he and his men had to hide in the sea king's cave disguised under sealskins—with insistent emphasis on their sickening smell (book 4.401 ff.). This tale, indeed, puts together a complex of motifs that appears with telling effect in the story of the Cyclops, but it also appears with some parts redistributed, in the tale of Circe and in the Odysseus–Eumaeus relationship: that complex is the linkage of animal disguise with guesthood, where the guest needs to overcome the host and win some sort of cooperation from him or them, whether unwilling or only bemused. The Wanderings of course give the theme of the disguised guest still more play and attention. In the Cyclops' cave Odysseus is disguised, first by his use of the trick name, and later by hiding himself and his surviving companions under the sheep, to escape from the cave and the now-blinded Polyphemus—thus he conducts a reprise of the animal-disguise theme, that of Menelaus with Proteus, and of the Greeks in the Wooden Horse. Circe, by turning her guests into beasts will constitute a different twist on this general theme: her guest-victims will be disguised not so much from her, as from other men, and from themselves, in a sense:

> . . . they now had the grunt, bristles, and skin of hogs but their mind remained the same as it had been.
>
> (10.239–40)

Thus they have two natures, one real and internal and the other somehow false but external and visible. They may also be said to represent the dangers that face a disguised guest; he may find his apparent and real identities split so far apart that they can never be reunited, or, like Odysseus, he may come to cling to the difference between the two identities and relish their separation in and for itself.

When Odysseus fails to react as Circe had expected to her drug, Circe is shocked and startled:

> What manner of man, and from where, are you? What is your city, who your parents? I am struck dumb that drinking my drug has not overcome you; for no other man has ever raised this cup but that he was instantly changed, once the draught passed his lips. You must have a heart that cannot be commanded in your breast.
>
> (10.325–29)

The drug, *moly*, given Odysseus by Hermes, is an antidote to Circe's drug, and thus makes him more than, and different from, ordinary men. To Circe his apparent human nature, given his invisible powers of resistance, is as sure a disguise as would be the magical change of his outer appearance by a god or goddess. Once again, and finally, in the Underworld, Odysseus is not precisely disguised (not by his doing, anyway), as much as simply, unreachably, and radically different, because he is alive. His difference from his hosts lies not in physical distance or different appearance but in their state of untouchableness (11.206–8). At each step of the adventures, some new form of isolation becomes his portion and lot, some new experience of the role of the noncomprehended man, the totally foreign monadic individual having no way of reaching into and relating to any form of community he visits. Much later, on Ogygia with Calypso, though they have been sleeping together for seven years, Odysseus' isolation has gone even further because distrust has now become systematic in him, and has displaced nearly all other visible traits of personality and expressions of feeling. On Scheria, and still more on Ithaca, distrust is almost a metaphysical mood. Moreover distrust, which had a rational basis when Odysseus was dealing with the Cyclops or Circe, lacks that basis when he is dealing later with Calypso, or the sea nymph Ino, or the Phaeacians. They are not unfriendly, but now he is incapable of revealing himself openly to anyone much less of accepting their good will at face value. Odysseus is not simply distrustful of the Phaeacians, he is anesthetized even to their random and innocent diversions, because he cannot really exist yet in any form of company. He is, in an important sense, now inhuman. Distrust has become its own justification, as though it were an art form.

So educated by his experiences, so isolated, so disposed toward other men—this is how Odysseus lands on Ithaca to reclaim his place as king, husband, and father. It is little wonder that the reclamation takes so long, half the poem, and it seems to be no accident that the poet or poets have designed the poem so that the length of time taken—and often objected to by critics—is in proportion to the depth to which the denaturing process has gone, on the general principle that serious illnesses take long convalescences. The poem seems to be telling one that a good half of Odysseus' labors and struggles, and perhaps the more important half, take place within a few yards, almost literally, of his and Penelope's wedding chamber, the supposed goal of all his aspirations, which he is so reluctant and wary of approaching once he actually arrives home.

It is obvious to the reader that on Scheria Odysseus was now assured of reaching home, in safety, in health, and even in wealth—and that the only task remaining was to rout the Suitors, a task such a resourceful man as he should not find too difficult. The Phaeacians, who were never really a threat, in fact duly dispatch him with gifts of great value on a stout ship for Ithaca. Yet, on the way, clearly no great distance, Odysseus falls asleep! (13.79) One should have thought that by now, well-rested (he has slept the night before, and such naturalistic information is seldom supplied in the Wanderings unless it has an ulterior purpose), rationally comforted, newly rich, and subject to normal anticipation, he might have stayed awake.* But the *Odyssey* is a poem that makes few concessions to naturalism.

---

* Aristotle, *Poetics,* ch. 24, was puzzled by this strange behavior.

Sleep in the *Odyssey* is used almost solely as a symbol of transition to new turns of direction in the hero's life and/or a new ordering of events. Although Odysseus like everyone else must sleep to live, sleep, for Odysseus himself, is mentioned only seven times in the poem, and all but one time, it appears to have symbolic status as a pivot—the only exception is the one mentioned above, where he sleeps the night before setting out for Ithaca, which seems to be merely natural sleep, and thus throws the sleep of the second night, on the boat, into contrast as probably unnecessary and unnatural. One may add that during the two nights he and his men spent in the Cyclops' cave, they did not sleep and spent the nights groaning (9.304; 9.436), while the giant does sleep, to his very great sorrow on the second night. Odysseus sleeps, otherwise, only at moments of crisis and transition. (This may be a peasant, or even childish symbolism, with night and sleep representative of leaving one world and entering another.) The first time, Odysseus falls asleep just in sight of Ithaca, whereupon his men untie the bag of winds given him by Aeolus, the event that began the really serious part of his exile, and in a way also foreshadows this occurrence, except that then his troubles were largely elemental while now they will be psychological. Odysseus sleeps again when his men slaughter the cattle of Helios (12.366 ff.)—which leads to their destruction and his last contact with human beings. He sleeps when he is washed ashore on Scheria naked and totally defenseless—this time indeed his fortunes will take an upward turn, but upon waking he does not assume that to be the case. In fact, each time, after the first, that Odysseus awakes he begins to fear the worst. And that of course is exactly what he does here. Finally he will sleep again, just before the contest of the bow in book 21, an adventure he has not sought and has tried to avoid, because, there again, he has nothing but misgivings and doubts.[4]

In the first two cases, sleep really did presage disaster. In the third it at least seemed to presage Odysseus' complete disappearance from history, as a household pet of the royal court of the Phaeacians. But now there is a new threat, or so it seems to him. He is safely put ashore sleeping on Ithaca, without treachery, by the Phaeacian sailors. But when he wakes he is totally alone in some kind of grotto that he, the king of the land, does not know. Even the treasures brought with him from Scheria, and scrupulously left by the sailors beside his sleeping form, do not reassure him, about their honesty or about anything else. He appears utterly dejected, fearful to the point of incoherence, and strangely lacking in the determination to do something, which had always been a mark of his character. To believe his own words, one would have to imagine that he suddenly has no idea how to proceed with his own interests. This, I suggest, is the poet's way of signaling that the most strenuous adventure of all is to come, the adventure within himself to open up his mind and identity, and to take the risks that returning to the human community will involve, not with enemies, but with his own people. Coming home, when either home itself or one's own perspectives have changed, can be a terrifying experience. Robert Fitzgerald in his fine translation of the *Odyssey* catches this sense of homecoming with the title he gives book 13 : "One More Strange Island."

In a moral sense Ithaca will prove to be the wildest and most dangerous land Odysseus will yet have visited. On Ithaca, he will find not monsters, goddesses, or the dead, but time distorted, emotions wrung dry, society upside down—all the product of his own absence, to be sure—but for a very long time he will feel alien to it all, and thus will be powerless to move in and set things right, because it is not really his simple physical return that is needed for that purpose. No longer—now it is not enough. His mere absence has indeed wrought chaos, but his simple presence cannot right it again, because the figure deposited on the sands of Ithaca by the Phaeacian sailors, at least for the time-being, is not a real human being, not a finite, limited, concrete individual with a living history, commitments, and liabilities; he is not a real Odysseus, only a potentiality, a possible husband, father, and king. As he is, he is only a bundle of negative defenses and evasions. For ten years progressive negation and withdrawal from "natural" human behavior has spelled safety. But these things have also "factored out" of his character all that is fixed, unique, particular, and especially important, time-bound, and have left behind only a set of provisional roles, abstractions, and false identities. Having learned all too well how to survive with these tools he has mislaid the personality that was to do the surviving. Having had to deal with nonsocial, nonhuman, and more or less timeless hosts for a decade, he had necessarily become a walking set of contingency plans, a blueprint for the theory of survival, who has ceased to be any particular man with those normal irrationalities, inescapable attachments, cherished idiosyncracies, and favorite desires, that in fact define a single human being. Desire, especially, that pure irreducible human will to prefer and to choose this rather than that, which compels almost all men at some point to refuse to bend or count costs any further, has been lost. To have a strong desire means to have a particular desire, to want a thing, a person or place, and to refuse to abandon it; it is to be human in the sense that to be vulnerable and threatened in defense of one's place is a sure sign of humanity. Odysseus has managed to avoid vulnerability and outwit threats, but the cost in humanity is high. Odysseus has to learn how to live again a human life that carries with it certain inescapable risks of being caught by unsuspected treachery and unforeseen threats. He is not yet ready for that experience, not prepared to cross that last borderline. Now the man of many turnings must be taught that the time of maneuver is over, that it is now the time for exerting strengths unapologetically, for claiming rights without disguises, and of admitting weaknesses without retreat. The strategy, adapted for all other islands and landfalls in the poem, of keeping open a line of retreat and leaving a margin of noncommitment, will not work on Ithaca, though Odysseus seems to take forever to learn that lesson.

No one denies of course that Odysseus has to overcome the Suitors, whom he finds engaged in a grotesque parody of the siege of Troy, here the comfortable siege of an anguished widow and even more of her pantry and cellar. He will also find the guest–host relationship shunted through a hundred mirrors to produce paradox upon paradox approaching sheer delirium. Odysseus is the unrecognized and unwilling host to the suitors, who in turn play host to him in his last disguise as a shipwrecked vagabond living in beggary. He will find that traditional heroism is dead, since he could hardly come bursting through the doors to confront the suitors like another Achilles, or so he thinks. He will also find the daily routine of the poor and ordinary elevated to a new importance that he will see for the first time, because he will have to share that position.

On waking up, Odysseus begins his plans by assuming, for no reason at all except the general conditions under which his mind now operates, that he has been deceitfully marooned by the sailors, and even after counting over his treasure he is not entirely relieved. While he is thinking generally melancholy thoughts and doing very little, Athena appears to him disguised as a shepherd boy and asks the reason for his evident mood. He relates his suspicions about the Phaeacians and then offers a totally imaginary account of who he is and how he has arrived at this spot. He claims to be a Cretan fleeing a murder warrant. At this point Athena cannot contain herself; she reveals herself and tries to bring him round by mocking gaily at his suspicious nature, urging him instead to press on with his plans:

> It would take a shrewd confidence-man indeed to get past you in tricky dealing—even a god would have trouble. Rascal, nonstop schemer, glutton of guile, won't you ever desist, even in your own homeland, from the lying tales and frauds that are your daily fare?
>
> (13.291–95)

Although, as is undeniable, Athena loves guile herself and cherishes schemers like Odysseus for just that characteristic in them, her main interest here is to stir him up to action, for she seems to realize that here and now still more sterile scheming is not the right strategy and indeed borders on an obsession. These particular suspicions and schemes will get him nowhere. At the same time, she seems either confused, or pessimistic about getting Odysseus to forego scheming entirely when she next counsels him to enter the palace in disguise, to trust no one including Penelope (though in the same breath she says Penelope is faithful), and to lie low waiting for a special chance to kill the suitors. Odysseus generally follows this line of advice in his subsequent actions—as the old Odysseus would no doubt have done—but neither he nor Athena seem to know now what those actions will be, nor *why* this stealth and circumspection will prove useful. It is only after Penelope suddenly proclaims the contest of the bow at the end of book 19, that all these elaborate preparations seem to have had some purpose. And it seems clear, as I will try to show in its proper place, that Odysseus had no idea the contest was coming, and indeed he demonstrates that he is not all that anxious for it to take place, once he knows of it.

Moreover, Athena's advice seems calculated to encourage just those characteristics of diffidence and guile of which she has just complained. In counseling a closed-mouth policy, in advising that he appear as some sort of vagabond, a neutral presence in no real way different from the Cretan fugitive he has just tried to impersonate, Athena seems to be contradicting her own very excellent advice of a few lines earlier. What, precisely, is her point? Why does she stir the plot still thicker by disguising Odysseus as an old and weak man, a disguise that adds little to the subsequent impersonation he gives as a sailor down on his luck, and even seems to conflict with it at some points? Again, as was noted above with the case of books 6 and 7, this may be the only way that he can be dealt with at all in his present mood, and she can at least inject a few practical suggestions, like the one that he entrust himself at first to Eumaeus the pig-man. This in particular will have repercussions far different from the considerations immediately understood by Odysseus or advanced by Athena as justifying such a tactic.

It was noted in the previous chapter, in connection with the adventure of the Cyclops, that the unique narrative gifts employed in the *Odyssey* sometimes work against the larger purpose of the poet or poets who framed it as a whole—at least with traditional audiences. The skill shown in the books of the wanderings, along with their naturally exciting content, has made them the best-known part of the *Odyssey,* such that we tend to know almost too much when we first meet Odysseus in book 5, and thus the sense of wonder it would appear the poet wished to create in us over the hero's diffidence and anxiety is dissipated. In the second half of the poem, perhaps, one poetic skill has outgeneraled another again. The eventual narration of Odysseus' battle with the suitors in book 22 is so vigorous and neatly drawn that we normally know of it ahead of time, and when reading the *Odyssey* in its proper order we look forward to it, and reach it forgetting just how long it took Odysseus to reach that point—eight books! Students and other impatient readers sometimes speak of the intervening books as mere filler, with the poet merely killing time, in order (perhaps?) simply to concoct a poem about as long as the *Iliad.* This criticism should be heard seriously, if not to agree with it, to see what it tells about the subtle differences between the *Odyssey* and a poem in the central heroic tradition like the *Iliad.* The latter poem knows how to organize a tale and make it meandering and majestic, usually by juggling different sorts of material —alternating domestic with military scenes, and the like—which it marshalls in a loose interlocking order that would be quite amenable to different orderings from the one that survives without doing damage to the general demands of the traditional saga or tale. The *Odyssey,* however, steadfastly resists interlarding this long stretch with more interesting material from the world of action, most certainly not because its poet is unfamiliar with writing action scenes, and therefore for some other reasons, which should be tracked down, if possible. (Moreover, this long section of the poem, if dull to some, is not in any sense loose.)

The theory that oral poets sang epics of the *Iliad's* general character and length to crowds at various local or international festivities over and over again down the centuries, eventually to produce the Greek epics now possessed as texts, runs into considerable difficulties if one were to apply the theory seriously to the waiting books of the *Odyssey,* for they would require us to imagine that a poet encountered a unique audience given to hard and serious listening that virtually demanded that he convert to slow-motion tactics like those found in these books, and that this poet or these poets rather quickly acquired a skill both demanding and strangely uneconomical in performing other epics, for whatever memory skills this section would demand would be unnecessarily fine-tuned for the performance of other epics—and would involve something close to sheer memorization of a given and canonical text, which is not how oral poets are said to practice. The point of these books, it seems to me, despite the blood-curdling scenes of book 22, which tend to block one's view, is that Odysseus, though now purged of his ancient loyalties to the heroic life, which is all to the good, as the poet sees it, is now so isolated, so limited in human sympathies as a result of his appalling adventures, so introspective and tentative as an individual (that is, so doubtful and shifting as to his own identity) that he simply could not reenter the palace and claim his former rights by any sort of frontal assault. Nor is it just the problem of the suitors; there are psychological bars to his reentry every bit as strong as the physical ones. In one sense there are no former rights, founded in the customary usages of the dead heroic world : he is in a new era in which a man must earn and deserve what he has or gets, and must make, quite literally, the place he occupies in society. Secondly, a more crucial problem : Odysseus must overcome and reconstitute himself—he must search out and embrace a new personality, new in the sense of being a complex of both the old Odysseus, buried for the moment under a mound of disguises and equivocations, plus a new person who can think, confide, and exchange truths in a new world. Indeed, the killing of the suitors, though posed as a narrative necessity, is hardly more than that; they are never a serious threat to him, and the almost comic ease with which they are dispatched—to forget for the moment the elaborate plans discussed anachronistically by Odysseus and Telemachus in book 16—indicates just that. The important victory Odysseus must win is a paradoxical conquest of the self : he must yield his by-now habitual slyness and mistrust, and make an acceptance full of risk, or so he feels, of the need to entrust himself to others in general, and to Penelope in particular.

I would argue that the last twelve books of the poem are anything but a hodgepodge of trivia and padding, a bad case of longuers from a poet who has lost the touch for the definite. Rather, the second half of the poem is a steady and profoundly sensitive study of the hero, shorn of his heroic—that is, auto-matic—signs of virtue and consequence, who is forced to reenter human society and climb, rung by rung, back up the ladder of both social and emotional dependence, before he can repossess home, wife, and property. He is being conducted here by the poet and by circumstance on a different series of adventures, a set of fundamentally more serious escapades than those of the Wanderings. He is being forced to learn, from the inside as it were, the whole of the human condition, its weaknesses and vices, its pleasures and strengths, as they are contained in his own little world of Ithaca, which were once unseen by him though they lay within a few yards or miles from the palace where he reigned long ago. Having passed through experiences unimaginable by any man, he must now pass through feigned conditions, as a beggar and vagabond, roles very real for certain men, but unimaginable to epic heroes, so distant are these conditions from their social rank and ordinary field of vision. The unsettling irony of the last half of the *Odyssey* is the fact that in a very real sense, any worthy man, no matter what his name or origins, on the day Penelope sets the contest of the bow just might have won her. Odysseus' last adventure is conducted by a poet concerned with teaching him not how to be Odysseus, son of Laertes, the old heroic formula, but how to be a trusting, humane, and sympathetic man, however anonymous, one capable of understanding all the possible conditions of human life because he has either experienced them himself or has been forced to encounter them and show sympathy with them. Odysseus' ten years of wandering commence with his claiming, in deceit, to be nobody; they end with his being forced to accept the risk of appearing to be anybody.

Upon his return to Ithaca and upon Athena's orders, Odysseus finds it necessary to entrust either his life or his secret, or both, in succession, to a slave, to his son, to the suitors when disguised as a beggar and freebooter, to the old maid Eurycleia, and finally to his own wife, who at more than one point must protect him with her authority. This is doubly wrenching. He who has come to trust no one, not even the gods, must now rely on just about everyone, including some very slender reeds indeed, at least as an epic hero would have thought. And he must do so just like every other dependent and unfortunate person, with at least the appearance of gratitude and subservience. The shipwrecks and beggars he impersonates are, by heroic standards, unimportant persons. How bitter it will be to learn by reenactment the fact that this world often errs in alloting station and merit to the opposite persons. Indeed in the heroic world of the *Iliad* it would have been something next to impossible to disguise greatness and hero status: the operative social ideologies in the *Iliad* imply that a hero would naturally refuse to mask his status and set aside the social dues that his status is owed at all times from all other men, for to mask status even as a strategem for a time would in fact make life meaningless and thus contradict the basic realities of heroic life; but still more, such strategems would not work, for heroic grandeur, it was felt, must shine through no matter what else may happen, and no one could really fail to recognize a hero when he saw one. All this is controverted by these books of the *Odyssey*, which force the hero to contemplate society, ironically a society he formerly ruled, from the bottom up. He is forced to experience almost every known form of social inferiority and powerlessness in the kingdom over which he is still at least the

titular ruler. Imagine Achilles or Diomedes or Ajax consenting
to appear as the dependent of slaves, of a boy, of a servant
woman, or even—or much less—of a wife! And that, simply
to survive, possibly to do no more than endure more and more
of the same kind of treatment, frustration, and humiliation
(since, of his own actions, Odysseus does nothing to bring about
a confrontation with either the Suitors or Penelope it appears at
least possible that he could swallow his pride forever; it is
Penelope's decree of the contest of the bow that forces his
hand). No Iliadic hero could have endured this situation ten
seconds. Any of them, in a similar situation, would simply have
burst through the front gate of the palace, shouting his glorious
name and title, no matter the consequences. But not Odysseus
now. We, and no doubt he, recall the angry regretful words of
Achilles' ghost, that life, even as the servant of a tenant farmer,
is better than death, no matter how glorious the gaining of it.
In his first step toward his return to real life, what does Odysseus
do but become the servant and guest, so far as any observer
could tell, of the slave Eumaeus, upon whom he must depend
for literally everything from food and shelter, information and
advice, protection from other slaves, to protection from dogs,[5]
and finally for a chance to see his own son!

Eumaeus is a kind of benign Cyclops, a pastoral figure,
close to nature and animals and possessed of a natural patience
inculcated by the rhythms of the seasons, a counterfoil to the
Cyclops, which represented nature's violent disregard of civilized
conventions, he represents nature's preference for real merit
versus socially acquired status. Odysseus on the other hand only
tells Eumaeus lies about his person and origins, and none of them
are in the heroic mode, interestingly enough : his stories all
make him out a wretched adventurer, a cursed loser in life, and
so he cannot expect the pig-man to worship him like a lord.
But for this sacrifice, he is rewarded : a new intimacy and
friendship arises—with his own slave, a man he has barely
known!—and a new revelation of humanity is granted.
Eumaeus, he now learns for the first time, is himself the long-

lost son of nobility, kidnapped by pirates as a boy and sold into lifelong slavery. Here is a tale even sadder than that of Odysseus himself—sadder than his made-up tales, too! Eumaeus' tale repeats and emphasizes the theme of the reversal of fortune, that Odysseus is by now so well acquainted with, and as well it enlightens the hero as to the virtue and history of one of his own slaves, with whom he forms the first real friendship, I believe, of the poem, and probably only the second or third in Greek epic.[6] Finally, the story of Eumaeus tells Odysseus that he is not the first or necessarily the best man whose real and rightful identity have been cloaked in disguise and hidden from the world of men by fell circumstance. The reeducation of Odysseus' emotions has begun. His capacity for sympathy has been enlarged, if only slightly—he is still suspicious enough to tell Eumaeus only lies—but he has at least taken the first few steps in learning an important general lesson, one that is true not just in his peculiar case, that virtue and merit are where you find them, but that men, while professing to identify and pre-serve virtue and merit, more or less routinely and predictably fail to recognize either of them when they actually and infre-quently occur.

At this point, the opening of book 16, by a seeming accident, Telemachus appears at the door of the pig-man's hut. The reader knows, though Odysseus could not, that Telemachus, warned by Athena not to land in the main harbor on his return from his fruitless errands to Pylos and Sparta but on the other side of the island, and sneak back to town in secret, is simply stopping by to greet his friend and confidant, Eumaeus. (Why the Suitors are pictured as a threat to Telemachus by sea, but not by land, is a minor puzzle of construction. The Suitors' over-elaborate preparations for the ambush seem excessive, by a wide mark, just to motivate this chance meeting in the mountains between father and son. The case could be made, persuasively, that the easy frustration of their ambush is meant to show the Suitors as ineffectual, and their inability to change their plan and deal with Telemachus on dry land may point to their essentially comic function in the poem.)

The meeting between father and son is tense and excruciating. Odysseus, who at this point has no mind to reveal himself to anyone, only agrees to greet his son when directly ordered to do so by Athena appearing in a special vision he alone can see. This portrait of his caution allows us, by contrast, to estimate his candid son's exquisite virtues. Telemachus is not a paragon of all possible virtues, but those he possesses are remarkable, not the least of which is patience and steadiness, needed at first for withstanding the suitors as best he could, and now for dealing with his father's eccentricities—for so they must appear to him—as Odysseus is now given to almost sadistic deviousness of speech and action. The scene is tense for another reason, because it shows Odysseus how, in contrast with his emotional distance from his son, Telemachus and Eumaeus express open and intense affection for one another. Indeed, the scene makes it clear that Eumaeus is the nearest thing Telemachus has to a father, as confidant, model, and guide. Odysseus is only a name to him—another sort of disguise, reputation, the well-known curse of the sons of famous fathers—plus a memory suggesting mainly backbreaking financial obligations and neurotic distress in his relations with his mother. Eumaeus, on the other hand, has been a real and reassuring presence and has in turn shown an unbought affection and concern for the young man, completely obliterating the vast difference in their present social standing—another reminder of the collapse of the heroic consciousness.

Finally, Athena forcing the issue, Odysseus reveals himself to his son, Eumaeus having been sent outside the hut on some errand or other, and after a moment's amazement on Telemachus' part, father and son put their heads together to plan a surprise revenge on the Suitors. In this exchange, Telemachus, not surprisingly, shows respect, intelligence, and attention toward this strange man, who impresses him primarily as a novel creature, but at first he seems unable to show any real affection for the man as his father. He is respectful mainly because he is an older man, and he is always respectful to such persons unless seriously provoked to behave otherwise. Indeed, it is interesting that unlike his father, even in a new and conceivably dangerous and doubtful situation, he feigns no emotions, for possible tactical reasons, that he does not genuinely feel. He neither imagines that Odysseus might be a trickster, though well he might, since he too has been hardened by having to endure some serious pressures and threats himself; nor does he pretend to feel a great wave of warmth and affection for his father, either, only reflecting the fact that hardly anyone could feel such emotions for a father missing from the scene all of one's remembered life. And it would be especially difficult with a father so inward and furtive as Odysseus has now become. Nor should we find this odd, that Telemachus, while son of the heroic world's most accomplished liar-for-policy, is probably the most candid and truthful character in all of Greek epic, a man of no personal policy whatever. Odysseus' problem, skillfully etched in this book as a kind of object-lesson, is now no longer really that of conquering physical threats or mental traps almost too formidable for even his ready wits, but that of dealing with real, limited, finite, and candid people, like Telemachus or Penelope, who have suffered their own special terrors and yet have remained attractively and vulnerably human through it all. Though Telemachus naturally and dutifully falls in with his father's plans and orders, that is only the result of his general piety toward his elders; affection, if it is to come, will only come much later. The behavior of Telemachus, proper and attentive but also reserved and diffident, is an early warning to Odysseus that the dangers of this last island, Ithaca, are clearly the opposite of those he has faced on all those other islands, from the land of the Cicones to the isle of Phaeacians.

The plans Odysseus and Telemachus make are complicated, and surely unreal, because their scheme to round up the armor hung in the great hall of the palace and lock it away has no tactical meaning here unless Odysseus could have known ahead of time that he would at some point find every last Suitor present in the hall and otherwise defenseless, while he himself would be present splendidly armed with a weapon, that is, unless he foreknew of the contest of the bow, but no one could know such a thing because Penelope will think it up only at the last moment. This passage of book 16 was written with book 21 in mind, and we can be sure as well that Odysseus had no such visions of the future at this time. This is probably one of the latest passages in the *Odyssey,* composed by a rather literal-minded man who found a technical difficulty in book 21 : why could the Suitors not have defended themselves with the ceremonial armor that is always hung on the walls of the dining hall? And this scheme was his lumbering, straightforward answer. (This suspect passage, while straightening out one difficulty, creates a worse one : presumably Odysseus' bow will have to be locked away with all the other arms—as indeed it is; Penelope has to send specially for it—so how could Odysseus assume he would be present, and be handed the bow by Penelope or anyone else, unless he knew about the contest and the fact that he, still disguised as a beggar, would be allowed to participate, despite the loud objections of the Suitors because they had not penetrated the disguise? This peculiar passage, if there is any merit in seeing it as part of the essential *Odyssey,* should best be seen simply as a vehicle demonstrating how Odysseus now makes slow-motion and overelaborate preparations—analogous to those of the Suitors scheming against Telemachus—against contingencies that even he can not imagine. It is a passage cut from the same cloth as his use of the name "No man" with the Cyclops, long before he had any idea how useful it would be to him.) Odysseus then adds a further touch, demanding that Telemachus not tell another soul that he is present on Ithaca, not his father, Laertes, not the swineherd, not even Penelope, because, he says, they must test the loyalty of the maidservants and the men who work the estates (book 15.300–307).

To deny Laertes the news seems sadistic, given the universal Greek obsession with having surviving children to perform one's funeral obsequies. And Eumaeus has surely already proved his loyalty.* And Penelope? On his adventures Odysseus had been subjected to countless reminders of the infidelities of famous women, and other analogies, like that suggested by the song of Ares and Aphrodite in book 8, such exposure had made him even more nervous about his own reception at home by his own wife, but all that was on the high seas, when he had no fresh information. Here, he has Telemachus to tell him whether or not Penelope is faithful. But no, he trusts almost nobody, and was not ready to trust Telemachus except for a divine command. Moreover, the reasoning he offers is a bit thin; testing the loyalties of servants and distant sharecroppers hardly seems connected with a decision to withhold his identity from his nearest kin—nor indeed is that loyalty really tested : Melanthius and some of the servant girls all too readily reveal their disloyalty, but not as the result of anything the Great Tactician has devised as a proper test, and no other real tests are applied in the text. Telemachus, who would hardly dream of contradicting his father directly, still manages to insinuate a note of impatience with all this deliberateness : he disagrees that there is time to test the opinion of every sharecropper, though he consents to some testing of the servant girls (this is not carried

* Eumaeus is addressed in the second person by the poet several times, *Eumaee sybota,* "Eumaeus, pig-man." This compositional oddity might perhaps best be explained by comparison with the possibly parallel case of Patroclus in the *Iliad,* who is frequently addressed by Homer as *Patrocle hippeu,* "Patroclus, horseman" (or "horse-tamer")—not that we ever see Patroclus riding a horse in the *Iliad.* Horses were associated with the nobility in Greece from the earliest times, because of the great expense keeping horses entailed, and names in historical times formed on the base *hipp-,* like Leucippus, Hippocles, Melanippe, etc., usually are taken to be claims to noble or royal descent. While I know no way of accounting for this strange form of direct address to Patroclus in the *Iliad,* the Odyssean formula *Eumaee sybota* appears to me as a sort of proletarian parody of that Iliadic formula. Pigs are obviously the sort of animal one associates with the lower classes, the direct opposite of horses. Perhaps the poet here is trying to emphasize the virtue and loyalty of the pig-man, degraded to the lowest rank of society, as the equal or better of Patroclus' noble loyalties toward Achilles.

out, since Eurycleia knows the facts anyway and saves everybody the trouble). Telemachus is humoring his father, but is adding, as best he can, a mildly sarcastic note of urgency—as Penelope will do later on—saying that it is hardly time to go counting noses in a kind of political poll on the outlying farms, while,

> . . . that luxurious bunch there in the house eats up our substance without thought of restraint. . . .

Telemachus urges his father to forego these roundabout schemes, his most characteristic mode of thought at this point, and to do something positive, and quickly! All this is set in ironic contrast with the events that actually occur in the balance of book 16 —the attempt of the Suitors to waylay and butcher Telemachus, not his father. It is Telemachus who is in danger at the moment, not his father, since virtually none of the Suitors can imagine that Odysseus is still alive. With something more than restraint, Telemachus fails to tell Odysseus of his own personal danger, and consents to palaver about the hypothetical dangers against which his father is laying almost preposterous plans. Yet the son is prepared to enter the palace himself in no disguise at all, with no protection other than his bold honesty, in order to carry out his father's plans, while his father has no intention of giving up his own disguises, and indeed he is already planning to burrow still deeper into them.

At the end of their strategy session, Eumaeus returns, and the three share a rustic meal and settle down to sleep. The next morning, the beginning of book 17, Telemachus arises with a firm decision already in his mind and upon his lips. He plans to force his father to aproach at least a bit closer to his own home. With a gruff air he addresses Eumaeus:

> . . . I have a task for you. Conduct this unfortunate fellow, this vagabond, down into town, so he can beg his victuals from whomever of the townsfolk wishes to share a bit with him. It is not my place to feed all men, with all the troubles I have.

> (17.9–13)

This superb little speech shows that Telemachus has understood the situation perfectly, and forces the action in just the right direction, by pretending to forget all about Odysseus' plans. If Eumaeus is not to know the identity of Odysseus, the only way to break his father free from the pig-man's rather comfortable hospitality, which could go on forever in perfect security with plots for an eventual return growing thicker and thicker, is a direct order from the lord pro tempore, which the stranger cannot countermand without giving away his identity, and so Odysseus is forced to go along with the quite different plan Telemachus implies in what is on the surface simply a housekeeping directive to one of his servants, and even has to do so with a good grace. He puts the best face he can upon the situation, and orates for a few moments praising the wisdom of the boy's idea and voicing general agreement that it is best to seek his sustenance in the town for the indefinite time he says he plans to spend on the island, though probably it all came as a complete surprise to him. Does Odysseus really want events to take this particular turn? No such specific plan was discussed in the previous book, and indeed at one point Telemachus had offered to send the still unidentified stranger a regular ration, plus clothing and a weapon as though he were to remain with Eumaeus for an indefinite time (17.78–84). None of this was even in the plans of Odysseus at all. This move on Telemachus' part is noteworthy because it triggers another stage in the reinduction of Odysseus into society, who will be forced by it to climb the social ladder rung by rung. With Eumaeus he is the dependent of a slave—virtually the same social position Achilles' ghost had named in book 11 as preferable to being gloriously dead; now he is subject to the authority of his son, a son who at the moment proves a good deal more decisive and direct than he is. He is being forced not just to see but to feel inferior conditions of life that no Iliadic hero, in life, could imagine tolerating for any reason whatsoever, certainly not for a cause so dubious as mere survival. Moreover, Odysseus is being subtly told by his son's words that until such time as he chooses to reveal himelf and take the risks such an action would entail, he not only will lack the ability to exercise his rightful authority, so-called, but still worse, with respect to the corporate reality of the house of Odysseus, as an unprofitable dependent, he will be no more than one more Suitor. Quite apart from his personal problems, Odysseus, father though he may be, while remaining anonymous, is no real father but simply one more consumer of a dwindling supply of goods and certainly no help to his son in stanching the continuous material outflow from his own estate. Telemachus has begun the slow process of provoking Odysseus to come forth from his shell and be himself again, a process that he and Penelope will have to continue for some good long time before it is successful. Telemachus obviously does not begrudge his father the food that is rightfully his (for Odysseus actually does all his begging in the palace, which means that he still consumes his own food), but this short speech also lets him know what his technical social position is and what it will remain until the time that he decides to reveal his identity, and the sense of urgency is not without its tone of reproach.

Notes

1. *See* book 17.484–86, for example.
2. Book 4.244–64; the story "swings" from a tale whose center is Odysseus to one that confirms Helen's protestations that by the time of the incident with Odysseus she was disgusted with her adventure and was anxious to return to Menelaus.
3. Menelaus' counterstory (4.266ff.) while also purporting to honor Odysseus, is obviously a retort to Helen and emphasizes the qualities opposite to those in her story : here she is pictured as giving the Trojans not just her continued loyalty but supererogatory aid that amounts to treason to the Greek cause, and she is therefore pictured as still unfaithful and lustful—by this time Paris would be dead and she would now have a third husband, Deiphobus, assuming that the poet of the *Odyssey* had the same version of the legend in mind as that which is known from later sources.
4. At Book 10.333 ff. Odysseus first enters the bed of Circe, though sleep is not specifically the point here; yet he does have some fear for his manhood (10.341, repeating 1.301). Obviously, Odysseus sleeps in Circe's bed for a whole year, but that is not really part of the narrative "line."

5. Book 12.29–47. These fierce dogs are a counter-image to the faithful dog Argus discussed below in chapter 3.

6. If Aristotle is formally correct, or even true to Greek thought in general, in thinking that friendship could only exist between equals, then the case of Achilles–Patroclus in the *Iliad* is not really a case of friendship. Patroclus is nothing more to Achilles than his most prized possession; if not a slave, still not a being capable of total free will or totally independent choices. As such, he is a kind of male Briseis, and it is interesting that Achilles, who drops out of battle over the loss of a woman, Briseis, returns to it over the loss of a man, Patroclus. The relationship of Briseis and Patroclus, on the other hand, may well be a case of genuine friendship—see her lament over the dead Patroclus at *Iliad* 19.282ff.—for the the two are each in his/her way equally subject to the moods and self-regard of Achilles, and may even both be subject to his sexual pleasure, if Aeschylus' suspicions as expressed in the fragmentary *Myrmidons* ring truer than the strange silences of the more circumspect Homer on this point. Aeschylus at least opens up an intriguing question. As collateral dependents of Achilles, Briseis and Patroclus are probably the first coequal friends in western letters. Besides this pair, I see few real friends in Greek epic, on the Greek side; on the Trojan side, Hector and Andromache, though husband and wife, seem to be friends as well, a situation seldom encountered in other classical accounts of married pairs.

3

The Last Suitor

ODYSSEUS YIELDS TO HIS SON'S DECISION, SINCE THERE IS little else he can do, and comes down from the hills to take his place at the manor as a kind of half-client, half-beggar. On his way he is kicked and abused by the goatherd Melanthius, who has curried the favor of the Suitors and constitutes a moral counterfoil to Eumaeus, the pig-man; but he shows the proper degree of servility: the abject and dependent should not be found displaying uncharacteristic shows of dignity or wrath after all, and he has chosen to play that role. Likewise, with the Suitors he more or less plays the down-looking unfortunate, grateful for his food and counting himself lucky that their abuse of him remains simply random bad manners and does not take on a pattern of concentrated hostility or serious suspicion—their carelessness assures him that his disguise is a well-fitting one. Even his notorious boxing match with the wretched Irus, which exposes his great strength, is one of the breaks in the disguise that always goes undetected, in comedy! In fact all the encounters he has with persons outside his own family in the last half of the poem are really comic in tone, including, really, his encounter with Athena upon waking up in the cave. It is essential in comedy that the hero be judged by his enemies as a weakling and no-account until the last possible moment —and some disguise, physical or moral, is the favorite device for leading them on in their incomprehension until vengeance has reached just the correct savor and ripeness. Comic disguises

100

fool everybody but the audience precisely because comic villains are such grotesque fools who exist only to be deceived. The misbehavior of Melanthius, the bravado of the serving girls and the Suitors, even the befuddled vainglory of old Irus, are all of a piece; they are those easily diagnosed and preposterously inept immoralities that comic villains routinely commit in order to bring their fate all the more surely and justly down upon their own stupid heads. Whether or not the fate of the Suitors, Melanthius, and the disloyal maids is entirely to the tastes and stomachs of a modern audience, it still is important to remember that the very excess of their misbehavior and the boldness of their talk turns them into lurid and empty characters[1] whose later literary descendants will populate melodrama and opera buffa.*

But there is an entirely different story to tell regarding Odysseus' relationship with Penelope throughout the second half of the poem. It is on this level where his final adventure really takes place, and it is a tale of real suspense and a special kind of terror. Penelope, for him, blends the roles of the dangerous female host of the sort he dealt with throughout his exile, with that of the loyal wife; while for her, he blends the roles of husband and devious, dishonest Suitor. Students of the poem have always commented on the hero's almost pathological reticence, about his identity, pointing to his savage reaction when Eurycleia discovers his scar and hence his true identity, the endless game of bluff and deception he heartlessly plays with Penelope herself, and even his sadistic treatment of his father, Laertes, if book 24 is genuine.[2] But because people seldom seem to read the *Odyssey*—perhaps I should say, scholars seldom seem

---

* The fact that the great battle of book 22 takes place indoors is, first of all, a comic reductio of the typical epic battle in the *Iliad*, and, second, a sufficient statement of the actual threat the Suitors posed to Odysseus, caught like greedy mice in a pantry by Odysseus as the business-like cat. The sheer exaggeration of his victory against such odds tells against our taking the battle with much seriousness. While a hero in the *Iliad* may be a match for three, four, or five ordinary men, the odds in this case—sixty or so to one—are comic in conception.

to read the *Odyssey*—as much more than a guidebook to the cultural trivia of an ill-remembered heroic world (the *Iliad* is the guidebook to the important artifacts), and a work with a nonsignificant plot, following the judgment of the ancient critic Longinus, who probably never read the whole thing,[3] they have made little or nothing of Odysseus' psychological state, still less of the fact that the most compelling and arguably most important part of books 13–24, is the struggle of wills between Odysseus and Penelope. If overcoming the Suitors were really the main point of the poem's action, then the poet responsible for most of the psychological-warfare conversations Odysseus has with various persons in these books, and especially with Penelope, constructed one of the most elaborate literary buildups going ultimately nowhere, in the history of literature, indeed in the history of any kind of storytelling.

The most important—and clearly the most debated—episode in these intermediate Books is less an episode than an argument among scholars whether Penelope recognizes Odysseus before he in fact declares his identity. But what is the point of debating such an issue, if one does not attempt to judge it in relation to the whole mass and structure of the poem and the dynamics of the story? Surely this particular question is crucial to any general theory of the poem's meaning, and, a fact seldom considered, some sense of the poem's overall construction should cast light on this problem as well! But no, debates about recognition or nonrecognition have gone on nearly in a vacuum, with the participants giving no glimpse of the thought on their part that the best answer to this question has momentous implications for the rest of the poem. Without such a thought behind it, debate on recognition becomes mere antiquarian play based on the tacit assumption that the poem has no special unity and a rudimentary and undemanding plot. The reluctance of so many scholars to make anything out of the second half of the *Odyssey,* or to search for anything resembling a plot, is part of this approach to the recognition question, which they so frequently decide in a total vacuum, as though the *Odyssey* were a museum along whose aisles one finds one delightful or amusing exhibit after another but with nothing to connect adjacent exhibits but proximity.

One must frame a new discussion of this old topic in such a fashion because the recognition question forms a very large part of this chapter, and I want to draw a distinction not just between my conclusions and those of certain other interpretations, but also to the *scale* assigned to the question. Those who have dealt with it as described in the previous paragraph have treated it as one among many mildly challenging problems in Homer, on all fours with the question why Achilles has two dinners at one point in the *Iliad* or why Theoclymenus is such a poor prophet in our poem. That, I hasten to say, is not the thinking here. The theme of lost or masked personal identity reaches its elaborately orchestrated finale with the question whether Odysseus reasserts his identity or Penelope possibly divines it beforehand. To determine which may be the case one must study most closely the symmetrical scenes where first Penelope seeks, and Odysseus repels, information as to his identity, and then Odysseus proclaims, and Penelope repels, the same. These scenes constitute spectacular pieces of evidence showing what the poem has been all about.

That Penelope does recognize Odysseus seems to be certain.[4] The recognition of Odysseus is a key to the question of identities, disguises, social place, and recognition of merit, the theme of this book. But in addition, the question of recognition is a key to the meaning of the second half of the poem, regardless of any special opinions this book may express, for on the question of recognition, and one or two other cruces of interpretation, depends the ability of the second half of the poem to mean anything at all.

As the opening lines of the poem foretell, Odysseus' fate will not be to do great deeds, primarily, but to survive and reach home, and along the way to have learned "the mind of many men." Both his fate and his knowledge will amount to the same thing and teach the same lesson : heroism and its code, if they ever really existed, are now dead, if only because of the passage of time—the general case; and, his own case, because of the experiences he has had, so many of which have forced him to reject and bury his epic personality for the greater good of survival and homecoming. Knowing the mind of many men is indeed the key to the hero's homecoming—which was never simply a problem in navigation; it is learning to play all the roles men are forced to enact, to experiences all possible fates involved in surviving, and just living in the world, and thus to expand one's sympathies, an excellent way also of curbing one's own spirit. (One way of reading the *Odyssey* is as a kind of maze game played by the poet against the hero, the former not letting the latter return home until he has experienced all levels of social reality, and endured the anxiety and frustration that are the fates of the many.[5]) Odysseus will learn to understand the message of Achilles' ghost : survival is its own good and and success is not a necessary condition of life—failure, certainly in the heroic sense, would do quite nicely. Teirisias, a hero of knowledge and experience, was perhaps the best model for Odysseus to follow. Odysseus will learn this not just from his own experiences, but from others, including his son, Eumaeus, the other servants, and even from animals. Both in his own adventures, and especially in those of the pig-man, he witnesses the power of bad luck to turn a man's life upside-down, making the slave the master and the master the slave, and yet life goes on as it must. In other words, his mind has been forced to move outward from the narrowly inscribed circle of heroic consciousness, looking always upon itself and taking its own measure, to encompass the experiences of other men of all sorts and kinds, something that Achilles in life could not have conceived of doing. Odysseus has learned, painfully, to trust and value men below him socially, and through the example of the noble Suitors, he will learn as well that social importance and moral worth are by no means commonly found in the same person.

But having been forced to play the inferior roles himself,

to live in a series of disguises, he has to an extent become those very many men whose mind he has been forced to know. Thus there is now a paradox in his own character. If Penelope seems to be urging him to make a claim to the inheritance of Odysseus, including herself, he must wonder whether that is because she has penetrated his disguise, or only because she finds him a reasonable facsimile of Odysseus and no longer knows or cares about the differences, if any? Is it a case of *Così è, se vi pare?* On the other hand, does Penelope make certain rather obvious gestures of invitation to him simply because she is desperate and he is the last resort, or because she really knows who he is? That is a problem of equal importance for Odysseus and for the serious reader of the poem. But, one may say, if Penelope knows who Odysseus really is, why does she not say so openly, but instead try to beguile him into making the revelation himself, and ultimately force him to do so with the contest of the bow? Does she somehow understand that until he can bring himself to make that revelation of his own free will, his personality will still actually be divided between Odysseus, the real Odysseus, and the creature of many disguises? Having experienced what he has, could one not say, Odysseus has now slowly to rebuild his original personality, minus the heroic reflexes that he had to shed in order to survive, and that this accounts for the agonizingly slow process of return to individual consciousness in the last twelve books? All these questions are involved in the seemingly simple question : does Penelope recognize Odysseus long before he chooses to reveal himself? Indeed, there is hardly a more important question to ask of the second half of the poem.

Penelope first learns of the presence of a new beggar in her hall (book 17.497 ff.) from overhearing his first quarrel with Antinous, the most self-confident and obnoxious of the Suitors, though she only meets him a good deal later in book 19.89 ff.). Following a peculiarly neurotic evening of feasting and insults, and after the Suitors have gone to sleep, the queen descends into the hall to accost the stranger and learn if he has heard anything of Odysseus in his travels. From his first moment home, Odysseus has poured forth a bewildering flood of lies about his past, to Athena in her disguise as a shepherd, to Eumaeus, and finally to the Suitors in book 17; this last speech, the one Penelope has overheard, like all the others, has emphasized a single theme : Odysseus has led a life of sea-borne vagabondage, traveling all over the map and beyond it. (As previously mentioned, this has made one acute interpreter of the poem ask whether the tales of Odysseus' adventures in books 9–12 were not fabricated out of the same piece of cloth.[6] The point is well taken, but I think the explanation would have to be more subtle.[7]) Since, she asks, he has lived on the sea for many years, perhaps he has run across Odysseus, or at least may have some word of him. But, true to the rules of hospitality, she first asks him to tell of himself, his land, and his ancestry (19.104–5), inviting the heroic greeting formula he had used with the Cyclops,* that led to so much further woe, be it remembered! This request, probably not of double meaning at this point, only calls forth a barrage of compliments : Penelope is as fair as the Sun, and her reputation for virtue is extolled in every nation, etc. (The only information about her virtue that Odysseus can know are the reports of Anticleia that Penelope is still a grieving widow, not yet remarried, and the highly ambiguous praise the leering ghost of Agamemnon lavishes on her in book 11. The latter effectively overshadows the former, both because Anticleia had not said that Penelope was a willing widow, and because Agamemnon met his end at the hands of a wife and a paramour not yet in any sense a declared husband.) Moreover, he says, she should not ask about him or his story, though he has been telling rich variations of it all over the island, because his tale is too sorrowful for words. Penelope replies to all this verbiage with a remarkably cool and frank speech, discounting any praise of her

* Since Odysseus and the Stranger are one, Penelope, knowingly or not, has asked him to tell of himself twice. A Greek audience would not have failed to note the extremely paradoxical nature of the words alone : the old heroic greeting formula turned into a mind-boggling identity problem.

beauty, and relating in quite logical order the dimensions of the difficulties in which she is caught. Compared to his rhetorical waffling and inexpensive cries of grief, her complaints are mature and pointed : she is a spiritual and physical wreck because her husband is gone and she no longer has the wherewithal to withstand the Suitors, lacking as well any help in deciding how to do the fair thing with regard to her son's legitimate interests in the residuum of Odysseus' property that still remains to them. Now she must do something definite. Time is important, because the property has shrunk to a dangerous minimum. Her duty to her son demands that she make some choice and leave the house, if necessary with a new husband, before everything is wasted and Telemachus is left with nothing. Even here, I suspect, she has begun to guess who he is. Her account emphasizes the sort of information that would go to prove she is a loyal wife, and in part her words resemble a message one might send to an absent hubsand, if his whereabouts were known (instead of a present husband whose whereabouts are unknown), urging him to return with all speed, especially the information that she must make a decision very shortly, in the interests of Telemachus' inheritance. *If* she has recognized him, then her account seems to be aimed at drawing him forth from his fables and fictions and getting him to reenter and defend his old place in the real world. At the end of her account she returns to her first question, who is he? And here, in its second cycle, the conversation almost clearly becomes something more than just a conversation, more than an exchange of information between two unrelated unfortunates who meet by chance, but a struggle of wills conducted more and more in elaborate code language :

> But you likewise tell me your ancestry and where you come from—for surely you were not born from a stone or from an ancient oak.
>
> (19.162–63)

The last phrase is evidently an ancient Greek proverb, quoted or paraphrased frequently in Greek literature,[8] meaning in essence that no one is without family and connections. But here the words have a flavor more than the proverbial. Rocks and oaks are, also proverbially, hard and unyielding objects, quite the opposite of vulnerable human flesh—or responsive human emotions. One may still debate at this point whether Penelope suspects the Stranger for who he is, but we can at least see that her words are in fact a proper account of his unfeeling treatment of her, whether or not she knows that just yet. His response to this is to groan mightily over the sadness of his tale, and then to tell it again—as one more variant on the tales he has told Athena, Eumaeus, and the Suitors—just one more Cretan lie, added to all the others. But within the lie he says something that, while not exactly the truth, is certainly far closer to it than anything he has said so far. Making a marginal concession to Penelope, he tells her a story of Odysseus that is not true (that they met on Crete years before—an event that did not take place, obviously), but which, he hopes, should make her feel slightly more confident about her husband's eventual return. All the story does is suggest that the two men have had parallel fates (which may be as far as Odysseus is willing to go, at the moment, in returning himself to his real identity), and his use of it seems to imply that by the bizarre logic of bad luck, the odds that favored this vagabond's turning up on Ithaca, should likewise favor the return of Odysseus. As the poet hardly need add, this cruel reply only brings tears to the queen's eyes (19.203–4). Meanwhile, the poet does add, Odysseus sat stolidly at her side, betraying no emotion at all, "with eyes that might have been of horn or iron / though he wept inwardly—it was a trick of his" (19.211–12).

That trick is a very large part of his most serious problem, and I think the poet is very shrewd to give it prominence in this fashion. His disguise of his feelings and his real nature, his last and worst disguise, is beginning to tear his wife apart, and it no longer serves any useful purpose; he is in no believable danger from her and anyhow it is no longer danger, one must conclude, that makes him go on dissembling, but rather a too highly developed taste for the dissembler's art. One suspects that Odysseus now finds life easiest when it is wrapped up in a cocoon of disguises, and that noncommitment and noninvolvement are now his most natural modes of existence. His life, sad to say, now seems fully complete only when he is totally within himself sharing nothing and no truth with any person outside of himself. Or, perhaps, one could say that the real Odysseus has become a kind of religious relic or private totem that a long-forgotten taboo forbids him to reveal to anyone.

The whole story of the past ten years has contrived to make Odysseus divide himself from the outside world by becoming a series of disguised persons who are, on the surface, very much like Odysseus, with knowledge of seafaring, exile, craft, and danger, but not Odysseus himself. He has indeed attempted to perpetrate these separate personalities all along on every chance encounter he could, saying he knows of Odysseus, but that he himself is a different man. The adventure with the Cyclops had taught him the danger of being Odysseus (because of the curse) and the protection of being Nobody. On occasion that device, and others similar to it, had served him well and protected his existence. But now he must reunite those two beings into one real personality and it is not clear that he knows how to do it, or any longer actually wants to. The technical problems of managing the two personae and keeping them distinct though parallel has by now so monopolized his mind, it would seem that he has lost sight of the original purpose behind deception and disguise: to get home again and be fully himself. Once home, logically, his masks should come off. But that is not for him, not just yet. Once home, he seems farther off than ever. He is now obsessively other, and can not find the means to doff the sham and expose the real Odysseus.

At this point (hinting perhaps that he is a famous liar like all Cretans of still another proverb), Penelope asks for tokens. How does he know it was Odysseus he once met, what did he look like, how was he dressed, who was with him? The Stranger is ready: Odysseus' clothes of a decade earlier

are described, especiallyy a peculiar brooch, and he throws
in a sketch of the physique of the first mate, Eurybates.
This much is naturally accurate enough, though the stranger
tries to say that he has no way of knowing how Odysseus came
by those particular clothes. They may not be the ones he left
Ithaca with. Penelope breaks down again—is it simple nostalgia
or is she hurt by his last remarks? Since Odysseus obviously
knows that she is the source of his embarkation wardrobe, it
seems sadistic for him, as the Stranger, to toss in such a point, a
chilling piece of concrete fact compounded with an airy pretense
of noninvolvement once again. And if Penelope has recognized
him, then the airiness is twice as wounding. After another siege
of weeping Penelope confirms that she knows the tokens and
then she adds :

> . . . I shall never welcome him home again to his own home-
> land. It was an evil fate indeed that took him off in his deep
> ship to accursed Troy.
>
> (19.257–60)

Apparently stung by the final-sounding tone of her refusal to
hope further, the Stranger seems to undergo a shift of feeling,
or perhaps only of strategy, and counters with a different tale.
But lately, he says, he heard that Odysseus was staying nearby
on the mainland, among the Thesprotians (19.269–72), and
that he is due to return momentarily with a great treasure—he
could have returned earlier, the Stranger adds, but was ashamed
to come home empty-handed (19.283–6). Moreover he himself,
the Stranger, only set out ahead of Odysseus by an odd chance
(19.291); but the master of the house is due home any day
now and she must show patience (19.300–302, 306–7). He also
swears an oath that this tale is true (19.302)! This is one more
lie, of course, but by this time, any reasonable reading of the
poem must conclude that Penelope too now knows that he is
lying, and has been throughout his stay on Ithaca. And in
particular, if she is rational, Penelope must realize that this new
tale, whatever its relation to truth, cancels out the earlier story

about encountering Odysseus on Crete. Her first question to the Stranger was to ask for news of Odysseus, and obviously it was fresh, not stale information she wanted. The Cretan story was an attempt to put her off, and to leave everything unsettled—he had obviously not been moved by her need to make a decision in haste in order to save the patrimony of Telemachus. But this new story is suddenly called forth by the apparent finality of her speech of despair, which makes him realize the problem of urgency. And, perhaps fearing that she may choose a new husband in the next day or two, it is a bid for time to make plans to rout the Suitors. It is also a small indication that he has made none so far and that the plan hatched in book 16 to remove the armor from the hall is a spurious later addition. In this episode, surely, Penelope must recognize with whom she is dealing. Odysseus was the proverbial trickster at the best of times, and now his penchant for deception and indirection has reached the point of apparent monomania. There are only two ways Penelope could now deal with the man's words: either he is Odysseus, who for some reason refuses to deal honestly with her all the while signaling to her that he only needs a little more time to mature his plans; or else the Stranger is only what he says he is, and his first story about Crete was just a lie to get into her good graces, while the second is a desperate attempt to stay in them at least for a fleeting few days more. At this point, apparently without premeditation, Penelope conceives her own plan, a reversal of Hamlet's one might say, and by directions tries to find indirections out. Speaking as though she has judged the man to be merely a stranger, a man with no connections to her, she makes a declaration that must force his hand, if he is perchance Odysseus, and not the Stranger at all.

Her next words in reply, paraphrased, are: No, stranger, Odysseus will not come home again—how I wish your words were true (19.311, the ambiguity is just right: his words are either lies, even if intended to comfort her, or false prophecies, which are as bad or worse); if he were ever to return, you, as a guest in his house, would then know the real hospitality that a great lord can provide when he wants to; but my heart tells me for certain that he will never return! (19.309–16). Odysseus, as sketched above, had divided himself into his real, but missing identity, and his anonymous, but present, disguises, and is struggling to maintain both as separate entities. He refuses to let anyone, even Penelope, either think that Odysseus is dead and gone, or to be sure just where Odysseus is, or when, in any definite sense, anyone will ever see him. He is playing his own equivocating Baptist to his own blushing and always evanescent Messiah. But Penelope begins at this point to force him to draw these two separated entities back together again, much against his will. Her remarks, then, about hospitality, are a piquant insinuation and a possibly intentional paradox : if you were present as the self-admitted Odysseus, what welcome you would give yourself as the wandering Stranger! Indeed her mere words, whatever Penelope's degree of enlightenment at this stage, carry this same force regardless. Penelope has indeed posed the precise problem, at once both social and literary : what happens when the two roles come face to face, as even he must know they will at some time? Clearly Odysseus cannot yet bring himself to face that moment when he must become again merely himself, and drop all the disguises and deceptions which threaten to become more cherished to him than reality.

In her next breath Penelope finally makes it clear that she has seen through the Stranger's disguise. In a sudden burst of will and energy she orders the servants to get busy and receive the Stranger with all the ceremonies due to truly important, noble guests : a bath, a bed, new clothes, etc. (19.317ff.). This, if not exactly the hospitality Odysseus could afford if he were at home managing his estates himself, is still a great deal more than a beggar and a shipwrecked vagabond down on his luck has any reason to expect, and is probably a great deal more than Penelope intended to offer a moment earlier. Odysseus refuses most of her offer (19.336ff.) but at least accepts having his feet washed, which provides a literary opening for Eurycleia's discovery of his scar and the famous digression on his naming and his early boyhood. Penelope seems delighted even by this concession from the Stranger:

> Oh my dear [or: my own] guest, of all my dear guests who have come from distant parts to my home no one has been so wise, or has spoken, as you do, with such comprehension and intelligence. I have an old servant woman here whose wits are about her . . . in fact she nursed and raised [Odysseus] himself, receiving him directly from his mother. She shall wash your feet, though she is no longer strong. Come, rise up, wise Eurycleia, wash the feet of him who is exactly the age your master would be now—for the hands and feet of Odysseus would look exactly like his do now; in hardship men grow old quickly.
>
> (19.350–60)

This speech is the crux of the recognition debate. Does Penelope's description of the Stranger as Odysseus' exact contemporary—and more, as a look-alike—indicate that she has recognized who he is? It must, though again not in isolation from other facts. First, this whole episode, from her sudden reanimation, after the Thesprotian lie, to her offer of hospitality, and through his refusal and the compromise of the footbath, was motivated by her obvious detection of a trick of some kind in the Stranger's information. Second, her sudden offer of hospitality on a gigantically increased scale from anything hinted at in the prior context seems obviously attributable to something she has inferred from his preceding words, trick or not. This offer would be an odd reaction if she were simply hurt or angered by the attempted deception, as though it were perpetrated by a real Stranger, but the offer is simply unexplainable if she has not noticed something. I think we must conclude that she is at the very least half-pleased by the trick: it tells her something that the spoken words evidently do not, and thus her sudden change of mental state from morose and desperate to bright and energetic. Note the word dear in the passage quoted. The word *philos* generally means "dear" in Greek of historical times, but in Homeric usage it more frequently means "my own."[9] Penelope's use of this particular word, twice, indicates, as does the suddenly munificent scale of hospitality offered, that the Stranger has assumed a new and far more important stature in her eyes. When the Stranger refuses all but the footbath, Penelope then delivers the words just quoted. And thus we reach a third consideration: if she has not recognized him, then her comparison of his age and general appearance with that of Odysseus is either somewhat silly, or else a bit flirtatious. (The latter thought, perhaps, occurs to the pathologically suspicious Odysseus, too: suppose she is willing to flirt with a mere Stranger? Even if that Stranger is Odysseus, but refuses to admit it, can the real Odysseus become jealous of the disguise he has himself adopted? I suspect he can. The lover who disguises himself to test his beloved's fidelity will become a frequent theme of later literature, though mostly on the comic side.) Penelope, in any case, when she chooses Eurycleia for the task of washing the Stranger's feet, delivers two pieces of information that would make little sense if all she saw before her were a Stranger completely unknown to her: first, that Eurycleia, though old and tired, and with dozens of able-bodied younger women about, will do the job, and second that she has always known the master, in fact from his first hour.[10] This last sets the stage for the long digression, as noted, but that can hardly be its only purpose. In Penelope's mind, no such digression or flashback occurs, of course, and her employment of Eurycleia seems to hint that while she herself may have sniffed out his identity, only Eurycleia can give it full confirmation, and if that should occur, why then Eurycleia, who has known Odysseus the longest of all the living, would be the most trustworthy person available in whom he could confide, since he seems unwilling to confide in her. The selection of the old woman is then an exquisitely tactful offer by Penelope to join in the strange conspiracy that she now must assume is important to her husband, though that too fails.

Before setting to her task, Eurycleia utters a spacious diatribe against bad luck and hardship, concluding with a remarkable echo of Penelope's insinuation about the Stranger's identity, if that is what it was:

> . . . But come, understand the word that I would tell you. Many guests have come here after long hardship, but I declare that no one has come who resembles Odysseus so closely in voice, look, and limbs.
>
> (19.378–81)

One may well wonder why she will need the scar to ascertain his identity! Moreover, this would be an odd and distasteful thing to say to a Stranger who is perceived as only that. Odysseus, of course, has an answer, but perhaps not as ready an answer as he usually has, and replies lamely: Yes, everyone remarks about our resemblance. This is weak and unconvincing.[11] Eurycleia has put the matter still more plainly than her mistress, but the tone and point are the same; the themes of hardship, wanderings, and the Stranger's physical resemblance to Odysseus. And the words, "understand the word I would tell you," have a kind of prophetic or oracular ring, inviting the hearer to look beneath its surface, though in this case, not much more than an inch below. Of course, Odysseus had invited all of this, by constantly concocting stories that gave the Stranger a perilous career on the high seas that sounded physically parallel and no doubt was meant to sound morally parallel, to that of Odysseus. The discovery of the scar, then, if read carefully, with the digression about the hero's name, is a revelation, not so much of his identity to another, as of his origins and essential being to himself. The flashback to the tale of Autolycus, the naming, and the Calydonian boar hunt, have been treated by critics in dozens of ways, but none has seen it as a revelation of his own past to Odysseus, to remind him that he cannot remain with a tentative set of personalities to choose from, that he must return, and rather quickly, to being one historically specific person who is like no other.[12] Upon discovery, Odysseus is in a rage and threatens Eurycleia that he will choke the life out of her if she should break his disguise. (I think Odysseus' anger is mainly with himself, for being found out.) As for Penelope, the poet says smoothly, Athena had "turned her mind away" (19.479) so that she did not notice these almost violent goings-on. May be, but perhaps all one needs imagine here is that Penelope consents not to appear to notice, just so that Odysseus might confide in his nurse, if he chooses not to trust his wife yet. Of course he does admit his identity to the nurse, since there is nothing else he can do, but it is not a real confidence, and he swears her to absolute secrecy; his disguise, he still desperately wants to believe, is still intact. Yet, as though she were now fully aware of both his failure to prevent the penetration of his disguise, as well as his failure to take the offer of confidence and come forth in his true identity, Penelope now returns to the circle of the firelight with a third new personality and a tone uncharacteristically harsh and bitter in the extreme. This is another Penelope, neither the weary pessimist of the early lines of this book, nor the briefly cheerful optimist offering sumptuous hospitality to a self-proclaimed vagabond who remarkably resembles her husband. This is now a somber fatalist, and decisive as only a fatalist can be:

> Stranger, one trifling question more from me. It is now the hour when the sweet bed calls, when beloved sleep enfolds a man, even when his heart is grieving. But some power allots me unlimited anguish. Though I almost enjoy my days of mourning, because I have the work of the house and servants to look to, when night comes, though it take all others to their beds, for me it will only stir a cloud of biting torments when I lie on my couch. . . . My soul is tossed hither and thither: shall I remain by my son and keep guard over all this that is mine, my servants and my great hall, honoring the bed of my husband—or should I follow some one of the Achaean suitors, the one who gives the best presents? My son, while still young and naive, forbade it, and told me not to leave my husband's house. But now that he is grown and

mature, even he says that I should depart from this house, grieving for his property, and all that the suitors are gobbling up.

(19.509–34)

Here the Stranger no longer earns the adjective *phile,* "dear" or "my own." He is simply that, a stranger. This speech means a very serious sort of business. It is no longer flattering and diplomatic by turns, as the earlier speeches were. It is a harsh recital of wrongs and the inability of Penelope to see her way to righting them in any way that will leave her with any happiness left in life. It is obviously meant to shame him into action, if it has any meaning at all. She dwells ambiguously on the matter of beds, both as places to sleep, and as the center of marriages. The Stranger—if that is all he wishes to remain—can now go to bed and expect sweet sleep and dreams, but she cannot do that. Her bed is the bed of Odysseus, who refuses to come home—in any sense that helps her—and reassert his claims to it. Paradoxically, her daytime tasks and worries are an anodyne and a form of escape. He may be able to while away the time reciting his allegedly past woes, but now he eats well, has no visible responsibilities, and seems utterly to enjoy himself making all those speeches about bad luck, which he has converted into an art form. She is faced with the horrid choice of remaining in a house which is rightfully hers, which she has served faithfully for so many years, in the interests of others, her husband and now her son, but indeed of watching the estate go bankrupt —or else of departing, with nothing left behind even to record her name in simple gratitude for all the services she has performed. The utter emptiness of her recent past and her forlorn future threaten her with an obliteration of her personality more complete than any ever faced by her husband. He at least is a vivid memory in this house—she will be nothing. She has endured one exile already, twice as long as his, to be followed perhaps by another stretching to the end of her life. In simple justice her claims to sympathy are greater than his, as they are in terms of personal grief and desolation to be faced for the future. I think it surely fair to say that at this point she now sees Odysseus playing the Stranger in the role of another Suitor, one more dubious and trifling adventurer, indeed the last and worst of them, who offers no presents at all, and raises her expectations with his tantalizing lies, while consuming her substance like all the others. Indeed, he is worse still, in that if he is Odysseus, he refuses to act as Odysseus, and thus fails to press his suit, the one suit she has obviously hinted that she would respond to.

To discover just what sort of Suitor the Stranger is, Penelope poses him a riddle in the form of an obviously made-up dream that a child could interpret. Moreover, just to make sure he gets the point, she then has the dream interpret itself. It is the alleged dream of the geese and the eagle (19.535–53). "But come," she says, "hear a dream I just had and reply to it": a flock of geese were eating grain by her house, when an eagle descended and destroyed them all "in her hall" (19.540). She cried out in complaint over this destruction. Then the eagle settled on the roof and spoke to her in a human voice: the geese are the Suitors, it said, and the eagle is Odysseus returned in vengeance. "But then," she sighs, "sleep left me and I saw the selfsame geese still feeding at their trough."

She had begun this speech with a vivid description of her own comfortless, sleepless nights. Mentioning a dream now, if not a fatal contradiction or flaw in the fabric, is still a fairly serious equivocation, if we think the dream to have been real. There are many material inconsistencies in the poems of Homer, but seldom within such short hailing distance of one another, and seldom so jarring. And I rather choose to think that this is not a dream Penelope has actually had, but one she desperately wants to have. She is also, in her way, telling stories, like him. Near collapse, she tells this concocted dream to a man who, it seems, could make it all come true if he could be coaxed out of his trance of otherness. Thus her almost snide words at the close—"I awoke to find the geese still feeding." In the dream she was sympathetic with the geese, and had to be told they were a metaphor for the Suitors, but now she speaks her truer mind and relishes the pejorative metaphor. This is the final and most important evidence of her recognition of her husband : she has exposed every weakness in her position hoping that this will finally entice him out of his emotional truancy to declare who he is once and for all, in order to regain his rightful place in his home and his own society. The imaginary eagle spoke in a human voice; the real man answers only in the voice of a seacat ready to disappear on the next tide :

> Lady, one can hardly picture the dream turning out diff-erently, especially since Odysseus has revealed how it will conclude. He appears as death to the suitors, every last one. Not one will escape.

> (19.555–58)

These words must strike Penelope as both unfeeling and out of focus. The death of the Suitors was not what she has especially desiderated, but the self-announced return of the eagle, who will bring rescue and consolation for her years of loneliness and terror. This may incidentally involve the punishment of the Suitors, though perhaps their dispersal would be sufficient, but her thoughts are mainly on reunion and security and an end to her role as a sleepless sentry. But Odysseus' thoughts are only on vengeance, which seems to be yet one more excuse for maintaining his disguise. He shows this by mysteriously and pre-posterously supposing or pretending to suppose that the eagle's human voice was literally that of Odysseus. It is a unique and quite ridiculous, reply. Though the Greeks were familiar enough with famous dreams in which animals or other symbols stood for human beings, nowhere else in Greek literature does a character suppose that the symbol speaking is literally the same thing as the symbolized person speaking, and certainly no truly innocent and un-self-conscious Stranger would make such a peculiar equation. This is just one last stab at keeping the personality of the famed Odysseus and that of the anonymous Stranger apart and separate to the end. He is still playing games,

and making circuitous hints that are more evasions than com-
munications, as though this were not Ithaca, but Phaeacia or
Aeaea, and he were dealing with Nausicaa or Circe. But
Penelope is beyond games. She is now in total despair. True, she
tried one hand at her husband's favorite game, circumstantial
lies: she made up the dream. That she made it up, that it
failed, and that she now has nothing left but the courage of
desperation is obvious from the suddenly grim and deadly speech
she now makes in reply to the Stranger, announcing the Contest
of the Bow:

> Stranger, remember that dreams are elusive and hard to
> interpret; they often fail of fulfilling men's wishes. For there
> are two gates through which unsubstantial dreams come.
> Some come through a gate of horn, others through ivory.
> Those which come through sawn ivory are a cheat and bring
> men false messages. Those coming through polished horn
> bring honest prophecy if a mortal truly inspect them. My
> dream, I am sure, did not come that way—it is just too close
> to what we, my son and I, desire.
>   And I shall tell you another thing—and ponder it well
> in your heart. This coming dawn is one of ill omen, for it
> will take me away from the house of Odysseus. . . . Now I
> shall set a contest for the suitors. Whoever of them easily
> strings the bow . . . him shall I follow, leaving this beautiful
> house of my bridal, though I shall remember it as in a dream.
>   (19.560–82)

Penelope, it is clear, is now beyond games. There is no more
time for her to play the Stranger's waiting game, any more than
there was reason, in her mind, to play the riddle game. The
dream was false, she says, not just because it came through the
gate of ivory, but because it was too close to what she wanted
—how better can she say she made it up to entice Odysseus
to reveal himself? It failed, and now all that she can do is to
take chances for the highest stakes at very poor odds. The
contest of the bow is an absolute risk on a totally uncertain
future, as she now sees it. Far from feeling assured by her

penetration of Odysseus' disguise, Penelope is less assured than ever. She can find no way to bring his two identities together, and must feel that he will take literally forever to do so himself. The contest is a last desperate cast to force him out of his costume and mask into the light of day because it sets a fixed time limit on his maneuverings, the very next morning! Though she is now quite certain that the Stranger is really her husband, that fact per se is steadily losing its importance and meaning for her. For an Odysseus who steadily refuses to identify himself, despite every sort of invitation to do so, is just a No Man as far as her view of her plight is concerned. The question for her is not the abstract one, Does Odysseus still live? or even the purely factual one, Is this man Odysseus? Rather, the question she needs to have answered is: Will Odysseus, or this man, whoever he is, lift a finger to come to her aid now (to his own aid, she implies, though she must feel by now that the Stranger is in no fit condition to understand this)? The contest of the bow is an ingenious, indeed an Odyssean trap, designed finally to entice the man Odysseus out of the theoretical identities he possesses as the Stranger, if he will ever come forth at all. (The Stranger, though as inventive as Odysseus, *never* invents a name for himself with Penelope.) Now he can no longer postpone his self-revelation unless he wants to lose her, permanently. He can no longer enjoy the game of dangling a variety of personalities and identities before her and others. It is also the last psychological opportunity he will have to rescue *his own* personality from oblivion and inconsequence, by taking a risk of his own, by settling on one personality and living out the one definite fate that a real, rather than a tentative, individual can have.*

* Penelope's interesting remark that her life as the wife of Odysseus, as long as it has gone on, will have no more reality than a dream once she leaves his house, is a searing indictment of Odysseus, if she has recognized him, or else a fearsome omen, if she has not. And, in either case, coming just after her celebrated distinction about two kinds of dreams, it must be meant, by the poet if not by herself, as a signal of warning and desperation to Odysseus himself. What, indeed, would become of his glory and his tale if the wife toward whom he has been working

Penelope had discerned the true identity of Odysseus in the Stranger. Why else, one must ask, would she bother to inform the Stranger of the contest at all? What would it mean to him, a Stranger passing through, uncommitted and unconnected with these events? Why should she add a second full account of her desperation as the reason for her decision? Or, if it may be argued that while she is almost certain of his identity, she is not fully certain, then the contest of the bow is a high-risk gamble intended to close the gap between almost certain and fully certain. She is willing to take the risk that she may be dead wrong, that this man may only be a vagabond from nowhere. By announcing the contest Penelope just might be consigning herself to another man, forever. This fact, one assumes, Penelope wants the Stranger to comprehend, with her words, "ponder it well in your heart."

Odysseus has immediate and severe difficulties with this new turn of affairs. To reply as she clearly is tempting him to do, he would in turn take great risks, at least as he sees it; he would risk exposing himself before he has concluded his own plans, if any, for his return, plus those suspicious schemes for testing the loyalty of everyone in his household establishment, a project that could take months if not years, especially for someone as constitutionally incapable of trust as he is. The contest of the bow is the final adventure, or so it seems, that Odysseus must face, and the one he has the least heart for. But one could also call it the final cause toward which all his adventures and efforts have been directed, namely to reach home and to say who he is. But having grown all too comfortable with disguises, he now seems to find that original end of all his efforts too hard and threatening for him to manage. Penelope's announcement is her last throw of the dice to force him to break free of his recent

his way for ten years, should renounce her place just before he is prepared to arrive home, consigning her marriage to the status of an insubstantial dream? The absolutely essential and distinctive mark of Odysseus as a hero has always been that he is a hero who has a fixed home and family, which are marginally more important to him than his "bachelor" exploits on the field of battle.

past and reenter history as it were, a real time, with its un-flattering limitations and obligations, its unexpected trials and unknown problems, and to leave behind that hypothetical time-span he has known and come to enjoy, of a romance lived in a disguise. But still, even at this point, where the slightest con-siderations of another's feelings would, one thinks, require that he reveal himself, he can do little more than make one more speech of anonymous reassurance, as though he were still a man quite outside the reach and range of events he is witnessing—this time, at least, he is a little more definite on the schedule of the hero's return, which is his only concession to Penelope's fear and hysteria :

> O revered wife of Odysseus, son of Laertcs, do not now postpone this contest : Odysseus the great planner will return before any of these fellows can take up his polished bow and string it.
>
> (19.583–87)

He tries to keep up her hope that Odysseus will return in time to head off the decision she plans the Contest to make for her, but still playing the Stranger, he remains uncommitted. The use of Odysseus' favorite weapon, the bow, is of course another attempt on her part to entice him into an admission; if she can not do it, perhaps the bow can, she must think. She pays no attention to these words and simply signals that the interview is over, appearing to have taken no comfort from his words, whatever he meant them to convey. By breaking off their talk, she seems to be saying that she must refuse his dubious comforts, in the absence of that which he owes her. She would, she says, enjoy speaking all night about her husband with the Stranger, but the gods have made it a law that all men must sleep, so each must go to his separate bed (19.589–93). Thus speaks the supposedly sleepless Penelope. She is not seeking sleep, one surmises, so much as relief from the heartlessly indirect and dissimulating ways of this baffling Stranger-Suitor-Husband. The irony is elegant : so long as he insists on maintaining the division in identities between Odysseus and the Stranger, just so long their beds must remain apart. Indeed, one may imagine that a new plot, connected with beds, is taking shape in her mind.

Penelope, by the strict form of the Contest, decrees that she will marry the winner. (That there will be one winner and not many is simply assumed by the folkloric origins of this part of the story; which is not to say that the poet has anything resembling the innocent intentions of folklore in using it here.) She has not said, by the way, that she believes the Stranger's prediction that Odysseus will return in time. Far from it, she says she expects one of the loutish Suitors to win both the contest and her. The contest, on the surface, is simply a way of solving the first problem she mentioned to the Stranger, that of protecting the remnant of Telemachus' patrimony, by allowing chance or skill to decide to which of a bad lot she will sacrifice herself on her son's behalf. The contest is not seen by her as a stage for the return and complete vindication of Odysseus, but only as remote chance for him to do so, and save her from the fate she would otherwise duly meet.[13] But how does it appear to Odysseus himself? We may grant that he has had at least prima facie grounds for not wanting to reveal himself openly and immediately upon his return to Ithaca. Perhaps he had some reason to suspect that his wife may have proved unfaithful and weak, and might even conceivably be preparing a trap for him, as Clytemnestra had for Agamemnon. Clytemnestra's infidelity, as Agamemnon's ghost gleefully reminded him in Hades, could be a powerful precedent, a precedent even worse than Helen's. He may possibly have thought, upon reaching the great house, that Penelope was flirting with him in his disguise when she remarked about his close resemblance to her husband, and made other moves of remarkable generosity toward a mere shipwrecked vagabond, which is all he claimed to be. Perhaps she has flirted with some of the other Suitors, too; or, if she truly loathes the Suitors as she says, just possibly she was prepared to jump into the arms of any man who resembled Odysseus, near enough to suit her, but not necessarily the real man himself. Was Penelope in effect telling the Stranger: whether you really are Odysseus or not, you are enough like him to suit me and my needs at this juncture, and therefore I will hold the contest; I both expect you to enter and anticipate that you will win and to claim me—in fact I am asking you to do just that; if the real Odysseus should appear, well and good, for he will either make the contest unnecessary by routing the Suitors, or else reveal himself by taking part in the Contest and winning; but if he does not, then I want you to participate and win because I am too weary for further struggle?

Such convoluted imaginings, of course, are the fantasies of a tormented and hypersuspicious mind, but lovers, especially those who think of love primarily as a matter of endangered possession, have such minds, and Odysseus has such a mind in any case. Does the beloved love the lover's self or just any reasonable facsimile? To a certain kind of lover, the closer the resemblance, the greater the torment: perhaps the greatest fear most lovers have is that the beloved will love a close simulacrum of the self. This, as noted earlier, is more often an explicit matter in comedy than in serious literature, though one must say that it also exists, thinly disguised in all literature devoted to loving and possessing, from this passage, to Shakespeare's comedies, to the sophisticated froth and nonsense of *Così Fan Tutte*. The problem then comes to this: Odysseus suddenly finds himself in a situation where his caution and genius for indirect action do not begin to tell against an entirely different sort of problem of surviving, this time moral survival, any more than the old heroic formulae could handle the problems of survival as he began his wanderings. And so, he must change once again the mental armor with which he has become familiar. A second redesign of his mental make-up is mandatory if he is to practice the art of survival through another and quite uncomfortable stage.

Having been taught, from the Cyclops on, that caution and

reticence make for survival, he now must learn how to take risks once again and assert the real lineaments of his true identity, flawed or defective or arbitrary as they may be, against forces that are arrayed against him on a battleground of their choosing, rather than his. He must now relearn how to gamble and take risks, the way the old heroes loved to do, though not for the same ends, nor with the same mental image of his deepest self. He must now gamble on the chance that Penelope wants him and not just a reasonable facsimile of himself. To the deviously logical mind, there can be no such thing as absolute proof of the loyalty and fidelity of another human being. The emotional world of real human beings is simply not open to perfect pre-assessments of emotional security, prior to the engagement of the feelings with another person. Odysseus has dwelt among nonhuman beings for the better part of ten years, and with them, caution, policy, and suspicion were all he needed, but he is now back home, among finite human beings, who neither stand in full command of themselves, nor expect or can tolerate total command and self-discipline in others who matter to them. It was all very well to enter the palace of Circe armed with science, tricks, and a sword. Circe understood and required that sort of approach, being a goddess. It will not work here. No one can fully protect himself from betrayal and loss when dealing with mere human beings, and still expect to engage in significant and adult emotional relationships with them. To an Odysseus, taught as he has been by his adventures to venture as little as possible and to work on the weaknesses of others while not exposing his own, the grave problem of reentering human society is primarily that of learning how, once again, to run sensible risks and behave with a human randomness and without over-wrought policy or plans. Close relationships, in his most recent past, spelled danger rather than reward. Just the opposite situation now confronts him. He is now simply too clever to engage in spontaneous human interactions with others, and he is hard put to understand how to change his ways. His last lesson, how to make the unguarded, uncalculated gesture of trust in another human being, how to risk and reveal himself bravely and without counting his tactical pennies, in the hopes of true fulfillment of his humanity, he has yet to learn.

Odysseus began his adventures by linguistically splitting his personality into an inner reality and an outer mask, and a peculiar one at that, No Man, or No One. That is, No Man with real human attachments, weaknesses and cherished idiosyncrasies. (Regrettably, I have no time or space here for a treatment of the strange way Odysseus in his various roles gives up, one after the other, that which I think men love above all things, their own special and peculiar preferences and tastes; on his adventures, while he not infrequently suppresses his name and his aims, he always suppresses his private loves and hates, and always seems to think, feel, and say what the occasion seems to demand in order to survive. He makes no unguarded or merely self-pleasing remarks that I can see. But this sort of leeching process makes Odysseus drain himself of all those peculiar angles and projections and singularities that we generally assume go to making a real human personality. The way is open, I thould think, for some other student of the poem to give this fascinating subject the treatment it deserves.) Returned to Ithaca, the hero's outer simulacrum, the negative and tentative personality adopted for so many tactical occasions, originally in defense of life and sanity, now of itself threatens to obliterate the inner reality, which is indeed not much more than a tiny guttering tongue of flame by the end of book 19 in any case. Odysseus is still a strong and capable fighter, a neat dissembler, and a classical survivor, but these are by now his occupations, and almost trades; the problem now is whether Odysseus is a human being with enough individual and scratchy reality to seem real to any other human being. Like a stone endlessly tossing for eons in the surf, he seems to have lost all significant individuating features.

There is no way to escape the final threat of anonymity and loss by making more devious plans. The only thing left for Odysseus is to fall in with the plan of Penelope, which is more whim than plan, and let himself be drawn into a course of action, designed by another, and without either full assurance of success or complete clarity, as he would like it, as to her motives. The announcement of the contest of the bow could not possibly settle any of Odysseus' still-lingering doubts, and if read a certain way, could be seen as increasing them. Yet it is the only field of action left open to him, as narrow as it is. Will he rise to the challenge and take the supreme risk, under conditions set by another? Penelope has now told him that he must be willing to risk as much as she is doing by seting the Contest, for he faces a potential loss almost as great as she does herself.

This situation as between Odysseus and Penelope is etched in vivid terms during the contest itself, when he first gingerly tried to string the bow, after all the other Suitors have tried and failed. Antinous complains in high aristocratic dudgeon that this beggar should be allowed no part in the contest. But Penelope lightly answers, and with bold and risky sarcasm, that as a guest (!) the Stranger-beggar has an equal right to try the bow, but that she would not marry the beggar even if he should be successful. This could be dangerous talk to the Suitors, who were capable of bloodthirsty if ineffective plots against Telemachus some books earlier, because it insults their social place and prominence and could fairly provoke further thoughts of mayhem against Odysseus himself. And, of course, it can be seen as still one more invitation seductively aimed at Odysseus to make him reveal his true identity. The subtler point is that she and the Stranger are already married, and would not marry again, no matter what the outcome.[14] The bow, the contest, and the subsequent battle in which Odysseus destroys every last one of the Suitors are in themselves matters of almost no concern to Penelope. She is sure the Stranger-Odysseus can handle the bow and defeat the Suitors—she is not so sure he can handle the difficult and dangerous business of resuming his own true identity and humanity once again. By means of the contest she had forced his hand into declaring himself to the household and polity of Ithaca in general, and had implied that, without such an open declaration he will be nothing more to her than the last and most distressing of the Suitors. But he must do more than that : without backtracking and evasions, he must declare himself to *her,* and not just in formal terms, but as a real human being, willing to stand firm and not melt into a thousand other personalities when confronted with the needs, fears, and indeed the angularities of another human being who needs his comforts, his assurances, and his self-commitments.

Everyone knows the results, the overt results, of the contest. After the ignominious failure of all the Suitors to string the bow, Odysseus easily strings it, shoots an arrow through that very peculiar target Penelope has designed, perhaps less as a test of his markmanship than to drive modern scholars mad interpreting it, and then commences to shoot down the Suitors. Telemachus and Eumaeus join him in subordinate roles, and together they bring the carnage to a successful and unanimous conclusion. Book 22 is full of blindingly fast action, disproportionate gore, and that remorseless self-righteousness that appeals to the preadolescent barbarian who resides in all of us to some degree. As such it effectively blots out from many readers' minds most of what precedes and even some of what follows, which is a great misfortune. The poet here has written a spicy bit of mock-epic scrimmage, and has enjoyed himself doing it—always remembering that it is an epic battle indoors, against helpless or near-helpless characters who are in some ways portrayed as mere comic chaff-villains.

But the battle is probably one of the least important acts —morally speaking—in the poem, and surely does little to solve Odysseus' really important personality problems as they have been sketched. The poet indicates this, both within the narrative of this book and in the sequel. Within the narrative, first of all, the victory against overwhelming odds is simply too one-sided to be taken fully seriously. It is not uncommon in the *Iliad* for a hero to wage an *aristeia* against odds of four or five to one, but there is epic exaggeration and then there is what one must call comic-epic exaggeration, for lack of anything else to call it. The *Iliad* makes its heroes out to be two or three times better men than "nowadays," as Homer puts it; its events take a longish bit of time—a war lasting ten years rather than the wars of perhaps one year's or two year's duration that Homer really knew; and epic riches are perhaps anywhere from three to ten times greater than those known in the poets' own day. But, on the same scale as Odysseus' *aristeia* in the hall, epic wars would last 100 to 300 years, men would compete for treasure worth perhaps 100,000 times anything known to the poet or poets, and conceivably heroes should be able to lift things forty times their own weight. Second, in this battle, the intervention of the gods, so frequent in a battle in the *Iliad,* is limited *to* Athena flying up to the rafters and perching there while she gloats over the slaughter below. Somehow this cannot be seen as simply an indoor analogue of Athena standing over an outdoor battlefield and terrifying whole armies with her aegis. A goddess perching on a rafter would resemble, to a peasant eye, a chicken or a turkey balancing on its roost for the night, and whether the *Odyssey* was composed for peasants or not, it is not unaware of how they tend to look at things.

Outside the narrative of the battle, the most important clue to the importance of the battle, is the fact that just before it begins Penelope retires to her quarters to go to sleep! She does not cower in fear or tremble with anxiety, she drifts away yawning, as though the whole thing is of almost no concern to her. Here, if we adopt her husband's estimate of things, is the most crucial moment in their lives, and it interests her so little that she of the long insomniac nights can not manage to stay awake to see the outcome! (Her sleep is remarkably like Odysseus' sleep just before landing on Ithaca after his visit to Aeolus: it marks an important transition to a new stage and kind of adventure, in this case for her. This, if nothing else, should make it clear that the poem's real moments of progress are moral rather than physical, and thus hardly heroic in the sense that the heroic life and career moves through a series of major external accomplishments, called *aristeiai,* perhaps the greatest one of them all. But it is not, and the sequel indicates that this is the case by the fact that there is no glory or adulation forthcoming to Odysseus for it; in fact, just the opposite occurs. Neither Penelope nor the guiding spirit of the poem was ever in the slightest doubt that Odysseus could take care of the Suitors—indeed the folkloric elements present in his revenge made that clear at even a more primitive level, to anyone who heard this poem near to the time of its origins. But it took the contest, with its threat that there was no more time for his schemes, that he must now fall in with her scheme, to make Odysseus come forth and make his bid for that which was rightfully his. The battle itself, then, holds no interest for Penelope and, rather economically, she sleeps as it rages on the floor beneath her bedroom. She knows full well that Odysseus will win that sort of battle easily enough. But there is another sort of victory to be gained, not by an isolated individual over one or more other individuals, but by a man over himself, and by both of them together, a victory of humanity and faith over suspicion and unnatural self-isolation. She had been driven to desperate measures only by his frustrating hesitations and regressive machinations. In stringing the bow and commencing the battle he did reveal himself, though perforce without courtesy, and with little attention paid to her real state of mind. That was something, but not enough; it was the old-fashioned sort of self-revelation, that of a conqueror, a hero, a breaker of things—what will now be needed is a mender of things.

Odysseus has to be taught two lessons about human beings before it could in truth be said that he has fully returned to his homeland; physical return and the discarding of his disguises is not, finally, enough. First, he must be taught that to be human in the new era with its standards so different from the heroic, he must be generally open to the possibility of risk and defeat, as much as to victory and success, for otherwise he simply will not be human. The old hero took risks, but his almost absolute self-knowledge nearly always told him what the outcome of each heroic encounter would be before it began. Each hero in the *Iliad,* for instance, knows pretty well whether the next enemy he finds facing him is his superior, his equal, or his inferior, and consequently he almost always knows within a narrow percentage what his chances are. The protestations about fate and chance in the *Iliad* have mainly to do with the situation prior to knowing who one's opponent will be, but once he is known, events happen in the *Iliad* with the logic of chess: divine intervention aside, a given figure, of a given power, before an opposing figure, with its given power, will almost always win or lose depending upon the foreknown ratio between the greatness of the two figures. Having won one more epic battle, however comic on its underside, Odysseus must be taught that the heroic standards no more work here on Ithaca than they did on the isle of Polyphemus. In the new world within which Odysseus wants to survive, heroic-epic certainties have vanished. But second, Odysseus must learn, though it is rather a process of unlearning, that life among the truly human is of no value unless it is spontaneous and reasonably trusting on normal occasions. For Odysseus to reveal himself in the great hall, armed to the teeth while the Suitors were helpless and trapped, to have the odds so grotesquely balanced in his favor, was neither a typical situation, nor any true index of his general willingness to trust knowledge of himself to personages he does not have so completely at his mercy. Odysseus must unlearn the lesson he had overlearned on his Adventures, and give up his perverse and convoluted suspicions about other merely human beings. To reveal one's self, one's name, is to reveal one's weaknesses, let us say, and to give others opportunities to do one harm. Giving up his name to Polyphemus earned Odysseus the curse and its attendant decade of wandering and pain. "Never again," one imagines a more prosaic Odysseus saying to himself after that critical mistake, but such a resolve is now precisely that which stands in the way of his returning home as a fully human and acceptable member of a human society. His experience of the nonhuman world, with its absolute, rather than conditional, powers of working harm, has made him incapable of comprehending simple human society, where, even if enemies abound, they are simply human like oneself, and all alike must eat and sleep and commit their share of blunders. Above all, to reintegrate oneself with truly human society again, one must resign the notion of maintaining perfect control over all modes and occasions of social interaction. One cannot carefully plan every interview with the cunning and elaboration that preceded Odysseus' entrances to the palace of Circe or the court of King Alcinous. On occasion other people, or mere circumstance, will dictate the prior conditions limiting one's behavior in a given social situation, and a reasonably self-assured and natural spontaneity, an uninstructed readiness to deal with other men and new situations on the basis of a general outlook toward life, must replace the fiendish and unnatural circumspection Odysseus has demonstrated heretofore. He must be taught the hard lesson that other men's acts are seldom so cunningly arranged and premeditated as his own have been for so long, and must learn how to respond without a long hiatus of planning and, bluntly, paranoia.

What is at stake here, essentially, is a "victory of weakness," winning by losing, at least as the inveterate schemer Odysseus would quite certainly view it, Odysseus has just won a contest that records a net gain in his sense of his own powers of command and success. But to become fully human again, he must come into possession once again, not just of his estates, but of his wife, a problem he had not foreseen in quite the terms she does. She is not to be his again, just because of one more *aristeia*, because such an act need not have left him any more inclined to open up his soul to spontaneity and human risk than he has been for years. For him to become fully human again, he must touch life again at all points, not just those of success, but even those of defeat or confusion. To win through to the finish line, as she sees it, her husband must succeed in being defeated by her, he must be administered a lesson in a situation in which she is in command while he undergoes a loss of command and control, over both the situation and himself. Only that can prove that he is vulnerable enough to be human. At some point he must learn the essential core of the message of Achilles' ghost : life is preferable to losing, true, but then it is equally preferable to winning, as well, whether what one wins is an epic battle that will be sung down the ages or simply the small wages of victory in verbal dueling with wife, son, or slave, if winning implies failure to make human contact or to maintain it. Achilles' ghost had declared that life, as a slave, was preferable to reigning over the dead. In the heroic world, kings were winners and slaves losers. A long moment too late, Achilles' ghost has seen through both winning and losing as all too frequently evanescent symbols in pursuit or avoidance of which one squanders life itself. Odysseus must be taught the lesson of failure, and Penelope must teach him.

I have noted earlier that for Odysseus sleep marks the boundary between worlds and situations and moods and turns of fortune. For Penelope, too, her sleep during the battle, the soundest in twenty years, so the poet says (book 22.17–19), marks a boundary. Whereas she was weak before sleep, she is now strong. Whereas she was a victim before, she is now in command. Whereas she was talkative and distraught before, she now evinces a certain strange wariness and taciturnity, which we are meant to see as the outward tokens of moral authority. She now has some serious teaching to do and a victory of her own to win. The Suitors were no real problem. But now that they are gone, she faces a man who is or might be a much more serious moral problem, and thus a man still potentially dangerous to her and himself. Not because he threatens her physically, but because he has yet to show sufficient signs of wanting, really, to be accepted back into the human race, to lead once again a time- and place-bound existence that is arbitrary and fixed in its conditions, not hypothetical and cancelable as the various "lives" of the Stranger had been. When Penelope is awakened, protesting, by Euryycleia, urgent and vociferous, telling of the defeat of the Suitors, she seems relieved enough to learn that they are

gone, but she now appears to doubt that her rescuer really is
Odysseus. In fact she states flatly that Odysseus is dead and
buried. She rattles on about the trickery of the gods and the
need for caution in dealing with a Stranger who has appeared
under conditions such as this, sounding for all the world like a
bitter parody of Odysseus himself in the last days preceding the
contest of the bow. Eurycleia is appalled—she, after all, had
seen the positive proof of the scar—Telemachus, too, protests
at her reluctance to recognize her lord, but all she offers them
is a vague promise to consider the matter further and to apply
some tests to the Stranger. Odysseus, who is present to hear all
this, stands up fairly well under this sort of badgering and
concedes her right to apply tests; he also offers the further
thought, a somewhat vulgar and smug one, that it is the blood
and battle grime on his person that make identification difficult,
and goes off to bathe and put on clean clothing. That should
make her recognize me, he thinks. But upon his return in
respectable couture she still refuses to acknowledge him. This
angers him and earns a reproof laced with rancor—Penelope's
moment is fast approaching:

> Odd woman, the Olympian gods have put in you a heart
> unfeeling, and strangely unlike your sex. What other woman
> would stand apart with such grim resolution from a husband
> who had endured hardship for twenty years and then
> returned home?
>
> (22.166–70)

How quickly Odysseus has forgotten his own lack of feeling
with Penelope, his own grim resolution in standing apart from
a woman who has also endured her own exile for the same
stretch of years. In response to this bit of barely controlled
indignation, Penelope just sits and stares, apparently. It seems
clear to her that these words indicate a singular failure in
Odysseus' understanding of much that has happened. In a move
of impatience and frustration, he turns to Eurycleia and orders
her to make up his bed—if he can not break through Penelope's

strange apathy (strange, to him!) and seeming indifference to
what has happened in the great hall, he at least wants his rest.
(The thematic irony here is neat: Odysseus has gotten easy and
instant recognition from some of his other hostesses—including
one he probably did not particularly want, that of Circe—followed in most instances by an invitation to their beds; but in
his true home, he has to issue reminders that he would like even
an unshared bed!) Then Penelope, as though slowly coming out
of a haze, says:

> Odd man, this is not my pride, nor is it contempt for you,
> nor am I simply beside myself. I know very well what sort
> of man you were the day you took ship from Ithaca. But,
> Eurycleia, get busy; do as he asks, make up his bed for him
> outside my chamber . . . which he himself constructed.
>
> (22.174–78)

These lines are packed with both surface and covert meaning.
The apparent slip of the tongue, "what sort of man you were,"
might simply mean, as the traditional commentators have
thought: you might be a god trying to trick me into an adulterous liaison. But that kind of reading makes the words bad
"theology" on her part and bad psychology on the author's
part. Penelope must have known that when gods set out to
trick mortal women into sleeping with them, they either win
their advantage through their power or their trickery, or if they
do not, that the object of their frustrated passion inevitably
reaps a miserable fate—one thinks of Apollo's less lucky loves
like Daphne or Cassandra. Penelope would know that no god
would make this sort of approach to her, huffy, bad-tempered
and querulous, nor, if she thinks this is a god rather than
Odysseus before her, does she act sufficiently impressed or
frightened. While many mythical women refused the caresses of
gods, none of them ever did so by bandying words with them,
as here. No. Penelope's slip of the tongue manifestly refers not
to her fear of being deceived by some god, but to a fear about
a man, who was once very different from what he is now. It

is his trickery and elusiveness that she is worried about. She is not afraid of being deceived by him, whether mortal or god, but of his own self-deception as to the real nature of human life lived with others, with whom one must share both strengths and weaknesses, both knowledge and ignorance, both confidence and fear. Her employment of the second-person past tense of the existential verb very cunningly sets before the reader and Odysseus the one real issue between them : he has been so good at concealing his identity, his own reality, from anyone he meets, that he has raised it to the status of a cherished ritual, and she is not at all sure that he is quite willing to relinquish it in the interests of rejoining society again, where the need to acknowledge one's own existence leaves one threatened and liable to all sorts of limitations, controls, demands, and threats. It had gotten to be too easy for Odysseus to safeguard himself with his disguised personality, so that he just might not want to return to the real world, where disguises are only for games. True, he has verbally identified himself as her husband, and called himself by his real name, but she has legitimate doubts that this means very much until he has shown some signs of really human and spontaneous activity that has not been thought out after long scheming. She needs to see the spontaneous act, the unpremeditated expression or the ultimate surd of the arbitrary self before she is ready to conclude that he is, has become, one might say, himself again. There is reason for her to fear that Odysseus' many disguises have served not just to protect his existence, but to hide his identity from himself as well. Penelope seems to be wondering if he, or anyone, has the right even to say that Odysseus still exists any more, since his essence has been parcelled out among so many feigned existences. You were such a man once, and that is how I remember you, Penelope says, but does that man still exist? You have taken upon yourself so many plausible roles—while perhaps whittling away at the real individual in the process—that you might be only the average of all the roles you have played, or worse, you might have no identity left at all, having tried to play too many of them.

The price of minimal survival might have proved, finally, too much. Has Odysseus lost his purchase on real human existence? Has he not given up too much in struggling over the seas, to be a specific human being once again, much as a rock or a piece of wood, fallen into the sea, only survives in the minimal sense by allowing itself to be ground down by the action of surf and sand until it is simply too smooth and symmetrical to suggest that life or individuality were ever in its possession?

Penelope's order to the servants to put a movable bed in the hallway instantly provokes Odysseus' famous outburst about the unmovable bed he had constructed in their bedroom, with one of its feet actually the stump of an olive tree still rooted in the earth. This is a test of sorts, as the poet himself says, indulging in perhaps the only piece of frank literary explanation in the Homeric corpus (22.181 : "She did this to test her husband."). But criticism has been just a bit dull about what kind of test, I suggest. What sort of test is it, really? Does she need to test his identity, by having him declare a piece of evidence that only she and Odysseus know? That seems unlikely since Eurycleia has offered the scar as evidence, since he has been able to bend the bow of Odysseus, and since he acts so fully at home once the battle is over. Moreover, it is impossible to conclude that she herself had not identified him long before the discovery of the scar. (It is the only way I could account for her actions just prior to the Contest, and especially for her hasty decision to set the Contest itself.) If Penelope is testing Odysseus for something here, I think it is not for redundant evidence of his minimal and technical identity, but for plausible evidence of his humanity. In other words, the testing is psychological : will Odysseus ever commit himself by revealing something in himself of his feelings and wishes and loyalties before making a full tactical reconnoiter of all possible threats to his security and telling all sorts of equivocating stories? Can "the great tactician" respond naturally to a challenge offered to his feelings, even if it means the loss of something he has come to hold dearer than his right to express himself, namely his tactical command of all possible gambits and confrontations? Will he risk the exposure of his feelings, having suppressed them for so long in order to purchase physical survival, simply because his human, private nature has been stirred? Above all, having won through to the security of his home and his rightful place in society once again, will he relax his guard to the degree that is natural in one's familiar and proper place, or will he remain distrustful and unnaturally canny to the end? It was, for Penelope, a narrow gamble, one must think, narrower than the contest of the bow, and more dangerous, but it works. Odysseus shouts:

> Woman! This is a soul-searing thing you have said! Who has dared to move my bed? A difficult task it would have been and one that took secret knowledge. . . .
>
> (22.183–85)

He goes on to describe its peculiar construction. It seems he possibly even thinks that if Penelope has shared the secret of the bed with anyone else, she may have shared it as well—he is still suspicious by nature. But there is this difference: instead of harboring his suspicions within himself and answering with mild and diplomatic words, reserving still more time for scheming and spying and testing of his own, he simply loses his temper and erupts in pure bluster, a far more natural thing to do for one who in fact feels that he has come home and has begun to experience an opening up of his emotional range and a greater security in expressing it. But that aside, his bad temper tells something else as well: he has been caught in a trick he neither devised nor suspected. Penelope has been able to reach a terribly well-concealed trigger in his mind and has made him react without thinking. Nothing and nobody had been able to make him do this for a decade, and he is clearly in a rage at being bested by his wife in a game of which he has heretofore been the master. For the first time in that decade he has reacted spontaneously and instinctively, and not out of calculation. Penelope has won a double victory: she has found a way to bring him home emotionally, and she has beaten him at his own game, which makes the victory better and sweeter for her. He is now doubly certified as fit to reenter the simply human world again, having expressed natural emotion in a natural way without calculation or forethought of any sort, and having experienced perhaps that most humanizing emotion of all, the crestfallen feeling of defeat, exposure, and frustration. For the length of this golden moment, he is neither Odysseus the long-dead hero of epic warfare, nor Odysseus the figure of subterfuge and roundabout prevarications, he is simply Odysseus the spluttering and indignant man. As such he is now capable of knowing and enjoying life in a new world, less splendid than the old heroic world, perhaps, but splendid enough for one who has had the rare fortune to survive at all from one age to another, because he has had the experiences that alone permitted his survival, and yet has been helped to transcend them too.

Notes

1. *See* L. A. Post, "Moral Patterns in Homer," *Transactions of the American Philological Association* 70 (1939): 159–60: "The morality of the plot of the *Odyssey* is indeed transparent. . . . In the *Odyssey* the hero and his family are nearly as flawless as possible. They are persecuted by suitors whose evil behavior is so emphasized that no reader can feel pity when they are slain." See also, C. Whitman, *Homer and the Heroic Tradition* (Cambridge, Mass.: Harvard University Press, 1958), pp. 305–8, and H. L. Levy, "The Odyssean Suitors and the Host–Guest Relationship," *Transactions of the American Philological Association* 94 (1963): 147ff. Levy observes that the "little" tradition, the folk tradition as distinct from the heroic tradition, would have viewed the waste and profligacy of the Suitors as heinous and dangerous, and that ignoring the value of goods consumed and the cost of their replacement was a kind of theft, and so the Suitors suffer condign punishment.
2. *See* D. L. Page, *The Homeric Odyssey* (Oxford: Oxford University Press 1955), ch. 5, especially pp. 111–14.
3. *On the Sublime* 9.13: ". . . the *Iliad* was written in maturity of spirit . . . while the *Odyssey,* is mostly story-telling, which is the characteristic of old age. Thus one could liken Homer in the *Odyssey* to the setting sun, retaining its size, but not its wonted power." What is astonishing here is not the notion that the *Odyssey* was composed by one of advanced years (which could mean nothing, despite Longinus' opinions) but that the poem is "mostly story-telling." Clearly, Longinus, like many modern readers, had read his *Odyssey* once, if at all, probably in his own youth, and has largely forgotten the real sequence of books.

4. Perhaps the best presentation of this interpretation is P. W. Harsh, "Penelope and Odysseus in the *Odyssey*," *American Journal of Philology* vol. 71 (1950): 2–3, 10ff. (I cannot, however, agree with Harsh that Odysseus himself understands Penelope's recognition; I think it is all one way, and that his reaction, which is not all that difficult for us to interpret, is rather the series of obsessive and suspicious subterfuges that one in fact sees him perform on the surface. Whitman (note 1 above), p. 303, also votes for Penelope's recognition of her husband. Disagreeing with Harsh in great detail, though, to me, not very clear as to her own view, is Anne Amory, "The Reunion of Odysseus and Penelope," cited from C. H. Taylor, ed., *Essays on the Odyssey* (Bloomington, Ind.: Indiana University Press 1963), pp. 100–123. In particular Amory denies that characters in Homer could withhold their private consciousness as Penelope must be doing if she has in fact recognized her husband; in Homer, she insists, characters may occasionally fool each other, but the audience, informed by the poet, always knows the truth of the situation. While it is true that Homer's expansive and repetitive style of construction generally permits him, if it does not require him, to put before us the hatching of the intention to deceive in a given character's mind long before the deception takes place, still I find Amory's absolute rule a bit too aprioristic for this instance. (And this instance is of course one of the cases that together must go to frame any such rule, which entails a problem of logical regress, if nothing else.) Also, as in *Odyssey* 4, for example, where Menelaus and Helen are clearly speaking their hostilities to one another, only under the surface of their language, there are other cases that shake if not over-turn Amory's "rule."

5. W. J. Woodhouse, *The Composition of Homer's Odyssey* (Oxford: Oxford University Press 1930), pp. 25 ff., observes that Odysseus met few if any real "men, after the fashion of this world" on his travels as actually related in the poem, that is, he meets supernatural or subhuman characters of ghosts, as I myself have emphasized in chapter 1. But the exordium of the poem, I have always assumed, basically refers to two things: the fact, however unimportant, that the Wanderings included more humdrum and unmentioned ports of call, at least in their initial weeks, than the hero chooses to relate in books 9–11 (see next note); and second, the fact, of immense importance, that the phrase "the mind of many men," refers to the many roles Odysseus himself will be forced to enact—that indeed he will have to *be* many different men, or at least is firmly convinced he must.

6. C. R. Beye, *The Iliad, the Odyssey and the Epic Tradition* (New York: Doubleday 1966), p. 185, writes, "The poet in so many ways raises doubts of Odysseus' veracity that perhaps the travel tales are but another in a series of deceptions. Here, the dupes are not only the Phaeacians, but the readers as well."

7. On the whole it would probably be better to view the travel tales as a partial psychological truth—as much of the truth as Odysseus will let himself recall and believe in. No doubt the ordering of the events, at

least up to the uneventful seven years with Calypso, represents a psychological rather than a chronological sequence.

8. *See Iliad* 22.126; Hesiod, *Theogony* 35; Plato, *Apology* 34d, *Republic* 544d.

9. The most frequent use of *philos* in Homer is for things that are physically part of one, the parts of the body or the *psyche*. Usage with respect to persons other than oneself can be illustrated by the first four occurrences of the word in the *Iliad*. At 1.20 Chryseis is called the "dear child" of Chryses; at 1.74, Achilles is addressed by Calchas as "dear to Zeus"; at 1.86, Apollo is called "dear to Zeus"; and at 1.98, Chryseis is given back to her "dear father." Now while "dear" might seem to us the proper emotional word here, it must be pointed out that Greek seldom has words for emotions or sentiments that do not reflect or affect the status of the individual in a concrete way. There is no way to refer to casual comradeship, idle flirtation, or momentary pique in the language as it is, for instance. In each of the cases referred to, "belonging to" would be the better, more precise translation of *philos,* because in each case some sort of blood relation is involved, the next degree of intimacy beyond one's relationship with oneself. True, *philos* later comes to mean what one means by "dear" or "cherished" but only for the rather obvious reason that a thing or a person becomes cherished because it is thought necessarily and irrevocably attached to one; so, too, the verb *phileo* was beginning to appear, meaning "to love," though perhaps earlier it meant rather to embrace or kiss, that is, to indicate that someone or something is *philos* to oneself because it was an intimate possession for which one would put up a struggle before yielding. One doubts that Achilles and Apollo were either of them especially "dear" to Zeus, in the English sense of the term—especially the latter, who was just then opposing his sire over the outcome of the Trojan War—but they both *belong* to Zeus because they are his descendants at different degrees of removal. And one may also doubt that it mattered much whether daughters like Chryseis were "dear" to the fathers—they were valuable property; nor would Homer or anyone else have taken much trouble to discover, or to care upon discovery, just what Chryseis might feel for Chryses; it did not matter if he were her "dear" father, in *our* sense, since he was her lord and master, and gave her title to her being!

10. It is true that Odysseus has asked for some old and trusted servant to do this service (18.344 ff.), but his reasons have to do with his fear, surely, of rude treatment by the younger girls, or some of them, which he has already experienced twice before (books 18.320 f. and 19.65–69). Penelope hardly appears to hear his reasons anyway, and her *stated* reasons for choosing Eurycleia are in fact a kind of riddle: she is old, and frail and overworked, but she has known the master from birth, therefore she shall attend you, the Stranger!

11. *See* W. B. Stanford's note to line 382 in his edition of the *Odyssey* (London: Macmillan, St. Martin's Press 1965), p. 331: ". . . with superb adroitness Odysseus, instead of denying the resemblance, as a less alert person might do, readily agrees, treating it as an observed fact." I must

say that I for one do not see this as a particularly adroit response. A truly alert Odysseus might have said something like, "Yes, and this resemblance got me into trouble once upon a time when . . ." and then have launched into a good diversionary story.

12. Erich Auerbach's famous essay on the discovery of the scar, in *Mimesis,* tr. Willard Trask (Princeton: Princeton University Press 1953), has its own special recommendations and marks of genius, true, but one must be troubled by his words, pp. 5–6, "The excursus upon the origin of Odysseus' scar is not basically different from the many passages in which a newly appearing object or implement, though it be in the thick of battle, is described as to its nature and origin; or, in which upon the appearance of a god, we are told where he last was, what he was doing there, and by what road he reached the scene. Here is the scar, which comes up in the course of the narrative; and Homer's feeling simply will not permit him to see it appear out of the darkness of an unilluminated past; it must be set in full light. . . ." But, one must argue, the scar hardly "comes up"; it is in fact *dragged* into a peculiar place in the narrative, where, as I have argued in agreement with many others, that recognition has already taken place (not just by Penelope but by Eurycleia as well, obviously, as noted above). The explanation of the excursus will have to be better than this, which is unfortunate, because Auerbach's generally fetching and imaginative study of Homer's style says many fine and memorable things for which he deserves great credit. Auerbach is surely correct in observing that, especially in the *Iliad* (this makes a crucial difference here) by and large, expansive and retarding digressions are frequent, and form a part of the whole style of the poem, as for instance the digression of the provenance and manufacture of Agamemnon's speaking staff in *Iliad* 1. But such things have no plot function, and the digression to the scar plainly does (even if it is not the function I have seen in it). Indeed, the scar passage may be both a parody of the Iliadic digression—as its sheer un-Iliadic length might indicate; compare Ovid's bloated mock-dirge over Corinna's parrot (*Amores* 2.6) with its parodic victim, Catullus' poem 3, a mere 18 lines on the death of Lesbia's sparrow —as well as having plot function. The *situs* of this passage, I am afraid, simply will not let us treat it as typical of anything else in the Homeric corpus, since it is absolutely unique. It occurs in the midst of a war of nerves over identity, self-revelation, and recognition; it spends a good deal of its time with an attempted etymology of Odysseus' name!; and finally, it anchors Odysseus firmly in the family of Autolycus, an inveterate trickster, liar, and troublemaker who hugely enjoyed his bad reputation. It presents Odysseus with a paradox: he of the tradition of tricksterism, while an anonymous piece of flotsam on his Wanderings, might very well have gotten away with his tricks without provoking too close inquiry as to his identity, but once home, where everyone knew both him and his grandfather, his continued trickiness only serves to identify him more and more certainly for the man he is, despite his every attempt to forestall that identification, for whatever peculiar psychological reasons. Here his most cherished resource, his trickiness, twists the sword from his

hand, for being clever and devious is the surest way to be recognized in this particular house and family.

13.   Woodhouse (note 5 above), pp. 92–107, deals most cleverly with the contest of the bow, but mainly with its folkloric plotting problems, merely, not with its long-range "motivation," as I would use the term here. Woodhouse assumes, (1) that there is no tacit schemes between Odysseus and Penelope (unlike Harsh, note 4 above), and (2) that "Penelope herself evidently has no idea that only Odysseus can bend the bow" (p. 93). He then goes on to explain why a double-contest is demanded, in a stage-manager's sense, because a mere contest in target-shooting even at an impossible target, would expend all the arrows before the Stranger should step up to take his turn, thus frustrating the revenge he "plots." On the other hand, a mere contest in stringing the bow alone need not be accompanied by any arrows at all, and thus again the Stranger would have no ammunition for his revenge, even if he were the only successful contestant. All this implies that same poet has thought out the physical plausibilities of the scene with some care. But my concern has been with the poet, whether the same man or another, who "motivated" the contest in the first place, that is, from the preceeding conversations between Odysseus and Penelope as described in this chapter. I agree with Woodhouse that the *Odyssey* was preceded by a more or less straight-forward "saga" on the return of Odysseus, in which a scheme between Odysseus and Penelope just might have produced the Contest of the Bow. We must then explain why the poet has dropped all that (forgetting to expunge another part of the scheme, the removal of arms, hatched in book 16 between Telemachus and his father, which has no meaning or justification in our present text) and has instead made the contest a matter of Penelope's sudden whim, triggered by something that happens in conversation between her and the Stranger, provoked by her own grim desperation and the Stranger's maddening, ineluctible evasions. (On this theory, the removal of the arms would not be a late bit of pedantry intruded into the poem, as I have so branded it above in the text of this chapter, but a fossil survivor of an older saga, which our poet has purposely disrupted and distorted in the direction of explaining psychological causation. I can not say which version is more appealing, but choosing between them still leaves my essential thesis intact, that Penelope does recognise Odysseus and on finding him impossibly evasive she therefore decides that it is up to her to force his hand.)

14.   This bit of word-play does not seem to have been noticed by any scholar I have been able to consult. I would defend my observation thus. Penelope's words, to the minds of the aristocratic Suitors, imply a recognition that an unbridgeable social gap exists between her and the moth-eaten Stranger, as is seen from the answer of Eurylochus, who prevents Antinous by answering her in his place: "None of us thinks that this fellow will take you to wife, since it would not be seemly; rather we stand in shame before the talk of men and women, lest someone should ever say of us . . . 'They were bested by a wretched beggar' " (21.322–28). But that is only one side. The peasant or "little" tradition would see

something very different in her words, since that tradition was responsive to the idea that the unimportant-seeming man would not only become important on the grounds of long-unrecognized merit, revealed in a blaze of unexpected glory, but might already be important, though presently in disguise. Strong wish-fulfillment surrounds this passage. But, besides, the idea that successful word-play allows the humble, unfortunate, or endangered to outwit and defeat their oppressors is also a large part of the peasant tradition. The victory of a small, helpless man over the Cyclops, through the clever use of words that mere power has never taken the trouble to master, represents a cherished part of folklore, and Penelope's witticism here is really in the same vein. Not only will her words contribute to her victory over oppressive and powerful men who are too busy in their own conceits to note her words carefully, but she has the additional pleasure of seeing her words, in and of themselves, constitute another sort of victory over the Suitors, for she has fooled them, not just defeated them.

4

The Artist in the *Odyssey*

The main fault of the *Odyssey* is that at many points the narrative content is drawn out to excessive lengths. At these points one feels that the monumental singer is consciously and almost painfully elaborating his material so as to make a great poem which will match the scale of the *Iliad*.*

IT IS USUALLY NOT THOUGHT BY SCHOLARS THAT ANCIENT Greek epic can be read for the subtleties this interpretation sees in the *Odyssey*. The reason, I take it, is that such things are to be found only in literature that is written, so that an author has the time to weave his special effects by having a manuscript always by his side and in which he can write and rewrite while pondering his subtlest points. For, if he could write, then he would surely have removed some of the adolescent errors from the text, the material inconsistencies and verbal contradictions that give Page so much amusement in book 11, or the mildly inconsistent twin versions of how the Cyclops live in book 9. The upshot, most think, is that the epics must have been composed in some nonwritten way, and must therefore be naive and not subject to authorial tricks or suggestions of any sort: the meaning must lie perfectly clear and upon an untroubled surface. And therefore an interpretation like this simply demands too much in the way of technical aids to composition that were lacking to the ancient poets.

* G. S. Kirk, *Homer and the Epic* (Cambridge: Cambridge University Press, 1965), pp. 115.

My answer to this involves a number of observations, some obvious, I should think, and some perhaps not. First, I have nothing to offer in rebuttal about the methods of composition that may have produced the *Odyssey,* or at least nothing of great moment. The theory of oral composition, though much is published about it, is only partially clear and as I understand it, it *can* account for a linear epic like the *Iliad,* which begins at the beginning and ends at the end. It is a little harder to see how it could account for the *Odyssey,* which begins at the end, or near it, returns to the beginning, and then takes its time ending again. But, if oral composition can account for the existence of a complex and subtle plot like that which I have discerned in the *Odyssey,* then I am perfectly prepared to yield to its champions. My interest is the complex and allusive plot, not the technical means by which it was fashioned, and it is that which I am prepared to defend, not a theory that the *Odyssey* was most certainly a written epic, for neither I nor anyone could know that, even it is would simplify matters if one could. What I mean by plot is a crafty device to broadcast a particular *version* of a tale along with an interpretation of its meaning—the poet of the *Odyssey* has been even more sub-jectively interpretive of the story's meaning than I have been—and not simply a monumental effort to record for posterity a grand story, whose essential meaning is left to make its impres-sions on its audience simply by the stirring effects of the telling (the *Odyssey* makes few attempts to stir; the *Iliad* many).

But can I prove my contention that the *Odyssey* is a firmly controlled plot, clearly under the direction of a literary mind intent on making subtle and non-obvious literary points that do not lie on the surface? Well, my "proofs" are of different orders. The most important are the foregoing three chapters, which demonstrate a well-knit literary intention and a masterly com-mand of converging theses, motifs, and issues. A major thematic system running through the *Odyssey,* and constituting perhaps its most striking unity, is that of identity, knowledge, disguises, and place in a society of other men. On the other hand, it is

proper to dwell on the matter of poetic composition and authorship, not to offer new theories about technicalities, but to show
that the poet of the *Odyssey* took the trouble to put such considerations before the reader's eyes in the very telling of the
story, and therefore they are part of it. The *Odyssey* comments,
in a variety of ways, on the nature and function of the poet,
glances at his relations with both his materials and his society,
and hints at the way one is to read or otherwise partake of his
accomplishment. And one of the most important things he does
is to quarrel, or at least differ significantly, with poets like those
who are now supposed to have composed the *Iliad,* in claiming
title to his production and making it relatively untouchable. At
least one poet who worked on the *Odyssey* took a lot of trouble
to get into the record his own view of what poets were, how
they functioned, what they deserved, what they knew, and how
they laid claim to public acceptance and reward. Since all this
is material found in the *Odyssey* itself, it is legitimate to include
it in a discussion of the literary aspects of the poem, both to point
out that the poet of the *Odyssey* disagrees with some of the
theorists who hold that ancient epic can only be a totally naive
repetition of a received story, and wants to assert title to, as
well as gain respect for, a well-plotted personal production. Since
the poet of the *Odyssey* has chosen to leave a record of his
literary ambitions, tensions, and anxieties in the poem itself, they
constitute part of the overall record and the argument that he,
far more than I, makes for viewing the *Odyssey* as a literary
document under the control of a superbly gifted, and pro-
portionately vain, craftsman, who demands that his audience
acknowledge his mastery and success. Indeed, just as one sees
the lower orders of society rising steadily if slowly through the
text of the *Odyssey,* one sees the poet, another sort of lower-class
figure, an artisan, rising to a state of self-consciousness and
demanding both literary and social considerations. Craftmanship,
a new sense of command over materials, independence, and
recognition are all involved in what follows; and they are

cleverly connected with the plot the poet has concocted, such that acknowledging the former means recognizing the latter.

While the plot of the *Odyssey* presents a situation in which social roles are disguised or confused with respect to merit, and the measurement of personal worth seems to rise and fall reciprocally rather than mutually with observable social status—while all this is going on there is just one instance of status-cum-worth that is becoming firmer rather than looser, and is rising on a rather constant curve, that of the poet himself.

By this I mean not just poets in the poem, but the poet of the poem, and as well the idea of a poet as a social and professional entity. It has long since been noted that the *Odyssey* honors poets on a grand scale while the *Iliad* does not, simply by making one of them, Demodocus, an honored minor character, and another one, Phemius, at least an intermittently interesting one. Both the praise Odysseus grants the former as well as the forgiveness he extends to the latter (for entertaining the Suitors in his house, but against his will) have been well-scrutinized by scholars for what they surely are, glimpses of both the ideal and the real in the lives of late prehistoric poets or bards.

But there is more to their appearances than a hint of technical information and very little notice has been paid to it. In the society of the *Odyssey* the poet begins to stand forth as the one dependable vessel of knowledge and unchallengeable skill by the relatively simple strategy of surviving his potential rivals, the priest and the seer. (Of course, another poet is managing all this, a point to which we shall return shortly.) By contrast, in the *Iliad* the plot is afoot when a man of power, the priest Chryses, calls Apollo's vengeance down upon the Greeks before Troy, and then a man of knowledge, the seer Calchas, very specifically warns those same Greeks of what they must do to allay that same god's vengeance, namely by pacifying the priest and giving him back his daughter, Chryseis. No challenge whatever is offered by any participant to either authority or their versions of the workings of the universe, certainly none by the poet of the *Iliad,* who seems as much in the grip of awe at the powers of priests and soothsayers as are his characters. Nor does the situation change throughout the *Iliad.*

In the *Odyssey,* however, a great deal has changed. Though the gods remain, at least on the fringes of the action (except for Athena), priests have quite disappeared and with them almost all vestiges of religion. True, Odysseus and his men perform a few routine sacrifices but there is no specially designated priest among them, and certainly no one with the power of Chryses. True, too, in book 3, one finds Nestor engaging in a huge and expensive sacrificial ritual, but again, there is no priest present, and one can imagine that the appearance of a real priest with power would markedly disconcert old Nestor, who is also, of course, a fossil of an age gone by in any case. Nor is there any thought for religious rituals, much less for priests when Odysseus returns to Ithaca in book 13, or even when he is reconciled with Penelope in book 23. But if priests simply disappear quietly, soothsayers, while they do not quite disappear, have an even more embarrassing time of it. D. L. Page is amused over the prophetic incapacities of one Theoclymenus, a misfit seer who stumbles upon Telemachus when returning from the Peloponnesus, and accompanies him home, solely to deliver a series of remarkably obtuse prophecies and interpretations of omens, which are probably not omens.[1] Teirisias in book 11 is consulted not so much for knowledge about the future as for geographical directions, though he, too, is a disappointment. The only other soothsaying that goes on is Odysseus' deliberately imperceptive interpretation of Penelope's (possibly false) dream. This dream, while possibly false, is reported along with its own transparent interpretation, and Odysseus' refusal to respond to it in the most obvious and natural way, it was suggested, only confirms to Penelope that there is something wrong with her husband, and triggers her decision to announce the contest of the bow. But, leaving aside the major momentum of the central plot, one could say that this passage on her false dream cast still more cold water over the science of the sooth-sayers, since her dream was probably a lie, no more real than Odysseus' tinny interpretations of it. So far had soothsaying fallen!

Meanwhile the poet has marched to the fore to dislodge seer and priest, and to claim a large part of their former scope, both as a residuary of past knowledge and skill, and as an interpreter of new events as well. Without being solemn or overbearing on this middle-sized point, I would insist that this displacement of seer and priest by the poet merits careful attention and suggests important guidelines for any interpretation of the *Odyssey* that hopes to avoid absurdity. The message, if quiet, is clear enough : the poet is determined to win status and respect through the vehicle of his work, and one neglects that fact to one's own critical embarrassment.

In addition, even if more than one poet had a hand in the composition of the *Odyssey,* he or they not only sing insinuations and advertisements for the craft of poets but make propaganda as well for their own social standing; besides this, one or more poets demonstrate in the *Odyssey* itself, a great jealousy for this very work, for the fabric of their minds and hands. This can be seen in the very way the *Odyssey seems to know itself* as a structure, a creation, a thing presenting itself as evidence that human craft executed it, taking glory even in showing the seams and joints where the toolmarks still show. In particular, the present version of the *Odyssey* seems to emphasize that it is an arrangement, a preconceived and craftily schemed configuration, or plot as a later era might call it, and not a natural or spon-taneous being, in no way natural and straightforward as are the events it aspires to describe. The poem also implies that departures from the straightforward, linear exposition of an un-folding set of events recounted in their natural order are due to an elaborate purpose, or perhaps even a message the poet has in store for his audience. All this is very different from the *Iliad,* which assumes, or at least pretends to, that the Muse takes on the major responsibility for telling the tale and that the poet is only her vehicle; that, further, any departures from natural straightforward order will only occur in reminiscences that certain characters would naturally engage in at crucial moments, like that of the aged Trojan councillor recollecting his first meeting with Odysseus in *Iliad* book 3 or Phoenix's recollections in book 9. The poet of the *Odyssey*, even if he is the same poet as that of the *Iliad*, proceeds very differently indeed. This poet enjoys showing the places where craft, for all practical purposes, has replaced inspiration, and will endure occasional embarrassments, as where a risky chance led to a botch, if only he can bask in admiration for other artistic dares successfully solved. The implausibly motivated trip of Odysseus to Hades, for instance, is well worth some of the useless speeches and other interviews Odysseus undergoes there, for the purposes of adding intensity to the plot and explicating his character. The occasional longuers of the Telemacheia or of books 13–19 are worth something for the chance to make telling points about Odysseus' lack of any identity in the real world, during his long exile.

That the poet of the *Odyssey* loves his literary tricks and even likes to call attention to them does not of course prove or even imply that he is greater than the poet of the *Iliad*, or that his work is greater either. But it does prove that he worked in a radically different mood and attitude of mind toward his materials and his characters. And it goes a long way toward proving that the *Odyssey* was constructed by a person or persons unknown who harbored ambitions much more recognizable as literary, than anything to be found in the *Iliad*. That difference is related to the subject discussed with respect to the plot and the characters, namely the question of recognition of worth by society: the conundrums about recognition and real worth that the plot propounds for the reader's puzzlement spring, at least in part, from the poet's own anxieties about his own status and the recognition accorded his craft for its merits, or not accorded, as the case may be. The poet of the *Odyssey* has decided to make his poem not just a competitive challenge to another epic, almost certainly the *Iliad*, but a private advertisement as well for the poet, his class, and his social function. G. S. Kirk in his book *Homer and the Epic*, and especially in the passage quoted at the head of this chapter, has observed that the *Odyssey* behaves as if it were standing enviously in the shadow of an already existing monumental poem, whether the *Iliad* or some other. One may also have recourse to the more intuitive testimony of another creative writer, namely, J. Giraudoux, whose wonderfully amusing *Elpénor*, a fanciful retelling of the *Odyssey*, displays numerous insights worth pursuing about the poem; perhaps most notably, an insinuation made in the song of the second siren to Odysseus that, having been taught by her the rudiments of the printing press, he should rush his adventures into print, and thus 'scoop" the *Iliad* or abort its very existence.*

The *Odyssey* is so peculiar in arrangement, so complex and indeed fiendish in outline that one must admit not just the silent presence of some other monumental epic against which it is reacting, but also the probable existence of an earlier poem, on whatever scale, which told the tale of Odysseus in a more or less straightforward way, analogous to the narrative line of the *Iliad* or other primary epic.

---

* ". . . la troisième sirène, la rousse, tournait sur son cap comme le jet d'un phare.
—— O Ulysse, chantait-elle. Veux-tu que tes exploits no périssent jamais? Conviens alors de signes qui seront l'image des mots ou des fragments de ces mots mêmes. Grave-les, à l'envers il va sans dire, dans une table de bois ou de cuivre, enduis le tout d'une huile noire, et presse ces moules contre un tissu. Si tu veus te venger d'Achille, ne traduis point son nom dans le métal, et il n'y aura pas d'Iliade !"
". . . the third Siren, in red, was turning on her cliff like the beam of a beacon.
—— Ulysses, she sang, Do you wish your adventures to be immortal? First learn those symbols that stand for words and parts of words; then engrave them, it goes without saying, in the reverse order, on a plaque of wood or copper; cover the whole with black oil and press them against a sheet of some material. If you wish to be avenged on Achilles, do not transcribe his name on the plate, and the *Iliad* will never come to be !"
(J. Giraudoux, *Elpénor* [Paris: Grasset, 1938], p. 68.)

The poet, it seems probable, then reworked this sort of material and tinkered together a vastly different and far more difficult organism that became this highly individualistic poem, even if longstretched, coming straight from more uncomplicated narratives. For instance, book 9.39 would have made a more likely opening for a standard epic on the model of the *Iliad,* and there are other possibilities, at the opening of book 5, for instance. But in such cases a poet operating with a simple linear notion of narrative time would either have contrived to tell the adventures, the present books 9–12, either as direct narrative in the poet's own voice, or as a more natural reminiscence, such as that of Phoenix in the *Iliad.* The poet, it would seem, tried desperately hard not to let either of those things happen, and made the problem as difficult as possible for himself.

Book 9, to which one must return again and again as the crux of so many issues in the *Odyssey,* is nothing like typical epic excurses in the *Iliad,* even if its introduction in the narrative, for a brief moment, echoes such epic excurses in an unnatural tone of voice. Unlike the Phoenix tale, the section on the Adventures is built on too grand a scale, obviously. Moreover, the opening of 9 would make a plausible beginning of an epic tale *except* that it is told by an epic hero about himself. The tale of Phoenix was a plausible digression precisely because he was a minor character : it made sense to have him reveal his history to those present in Achilles' tent, both because his story contains a moral point, and because there is no need to assume that anyone present, even Achilles, his closest connection, may quite know all of his tale. Major heroes, however, do not tell their own tales in standard heroic epic, because they do not need to. On occasion Achilles is discovered in his tent singing the great deeds of other and past heroes, but not his own.[2] The epic version of suspended disbelief implies that each important hero has a Homer to take care of his own tale for him. Indeed, this point is made in *Odyssey* 8 when Demodocus, not Odysseus, sings of Odysseus and other heroes and their adventures at Troy ! This is the public part of Odysseus' tale, and is quite well-known everywhere in the civilized world, as Odysseus reminds all present when he begins his own tale of that part of his life that is known, till that point, by no completely human being still left alive at all.

But if book 9 had been the opening of an earlier and conventional epic of Odysseus, then almost certainly it would have begun with the present line 39, where the tale of the Adventures actually commences. The first two-score lines of the book appear quite clearly as some sort of stitching whereby the original opening of the older, hypothetical poem is attached to the unit we now know as books 1–8. One evidence of such stitching is the brief reference Odysseus makes to his sexual liaisons with Circe and Calypso, more or less unwilling—or so he says—as they were (lines 29–33). (These references, by the way, are made in an order the reverse of their "real" occurrences in the narrative of the Adventures. Odysseus met Circe before meeting Calypso, but mentions Calypso before mentioning Circe—just as the poem in its present version does!—one small clue to self-consciousness of the author and of his concern for a convoluted plot.) These lines are an attempt to tie the early, naive, and unselfconsciously "epic" opening of the Adventures to the present structure, referring both backward to the narrative of Calypso in book 5, and forward to the narrative of Circe in books 10 and 11, while reminding those who can keep up with him, that the poet has in fact made these two incidents take place before our eyes in the reverse order of their "real" happening.

Naturally, this sort of maneuver is of vital interest in any study of the poem's construction, but for the moment let us concentrate on something even more revealing, and much more startling about the first thirty-nine lines of stitching at the opening of book 9. The first eighteen lines of the book show, for the first time (and for the last time, except for *Aeneid* 2–3, which is a conventional gesture of homage to the *Odyssey* in this respect, though great poetry for very different reasons[3]), an "epic" hero preparing to sing of his own past deeds almost as though they were a mere tale, a piece of the past which happened, almost, to someone else. A recitation of historical facts, irrevocable, and perhaps irrelevant, because they tell of a world that no longer exists, perhaps never existed, and of events that happened to a man who may not exist himself any longer, or at least he has large suspicions about the precise conditions of his existence. Moreover, that hero, that former hero one might say, is now converted into a poet, and by another poet! Suddenly and for a brief moment, the social distance between the hero and the bard is collapsed. The bard, who had formerly to rest content with celebrating anonymously the deeds of great man of brawn and action, men who would have disdained to meet a bard in private, real life, except in the most perfunctory way, now suddenly has the momentous opportunity to blend his personality and status with the hero himself! To set the scene the poet first rather pointedly has Odysseus praise the skill of the court poet Demodocus, who has just finished entertaining the feasters in Alcinous' hall, and then, when introducing his own tale, has him ask,

What shall I tell at the beginning, and what keep back for last?

(8.14)

That is, shall I tell my tale back-to-front or front-to-back? The hero of the tale, now that he has become its teller, and thus a poet, is suddenly faced with a literary problem to solve. Implicit in his words is the thesis that the natural order of events is not necessarily the optimal literary sequence, and indeed may have no specific value or merit at all. A teller of tales, these words say, must make what is essentially an artistic choice of sequence and means. Now it turns out that Odysseus tells his tale front-to-back, in the natural chronological order, so far as the reader can tell. But the line quoted seems to be a device to remind us that the poet who is presiding over the entire scene, and pulling the strings on his characters, including the new hero-become-poet Odysseus, has told his tale up to this point in

reverse order or back-to-front: the events of *Odyssey* 1–8 are
a backward-reeling cinema.

The hero-poet's opening words propel one to another insight
as well: the poet is now trying somehow to associate his art with
the *arete,* the heroic achievements, of Odysseus, simply by
having him—indeed, forcing him—to condescend to worry
about a poet's problems. Just moments before, Odysseus had
praised Demodocus for his skill and called it a rare gift, and
now we see him beginning to experience the pressure, and
perhaps the satisfaction too, of artistic competition. This, one
must think, was a rare piece of arrogance or contentiousness on
the part of mere bard, to claim near-equality with a hero.
Moreover this arrogance, if that is what to call it, soon appears
again. In book 10, when Odysseus' tale is broken for a night's
rest, King Alcinous declares:

> You have told your tale truly, knowledgeably, like a bard.
> (10.368)

Once again the poet, who controls all the events, seeks to close
the distance between the man of action, the hero, and the poet,
who is the man fitted to know what it is that makes a hero,
and indeed himself makes the hero by singing his praises. Without the poet to sing his deeds a hero's career would not outlast
him—so the poet implies. How very different the view of the
Iliad—if one recalls the scene where Achilles is discovered in
his tent singing the praise of great men of the past: the earlier
poem seems to assume that great deeds will simply force themselves into song that is automatically available for other men to
sing[4]—the poet knows a different story and wants his audience
to know it, too.

One might say that with the king's words Odysseus has just
mastered the art of the bard. The king of course has granted
it formally, but it is the poet, behind all the actions, who has
managed the words so that he can grant himself something still
better and more imposing: recognition and status competitive
even with that of the hero, especially because of his knowledge.

We have already seen that knowledge, in the *Odyssey,* is the replacement virtue for the old heroic, and Iliadic, virtue of courage.

The reannouncement of this theme—linking poet and hero in a special, if momentary, fraternity of knowledge transcending social barriers—is echoed at a climactic moment in the poem, when Odysseus takes his turn during the contest of the bow. Here at a moment when Odysseus makes the first positive move toward reclaiming his position as lord, husband and father, the poet takes the occasion to praise not his physical courage but his knowledge, and to compare that virtue of the hero's with, again, the virtue of a poet:

> . . . then complex Odysseus took the great bow in his hands, hefted it and inspected it closely, and, just like a man skilled with the harp and the ways of song who easily stretches a new string to the pegs of his instrument, so he took the sheepgut string in both hands and effortlessly strung the great bow. With his right hand he plucked the string and it sang out a fair note like a swallow's call.
>
> (21.404–11)

Here, in one of the rather rare similes in the *Odyssey,* at a moment of high drama and just before the only battle writing in the poem, the hero must borrow his metaphorical plumage from his poet, his own creator. The farfetched simile, though common enough in the *Iliad,* is never simultaneously suppositious and leading; it does not attempt to guide or coax the reader (hearer) into a certain view of the moral dispositions of the characters to whom the figures in the simile are being compared, much less to coerce from him a certain literary interpretation of the poet's motives in using the given simile. Something much more serious and complex is at work here, especially because the simile refers to a craft—that is common in the *Iliad*—not to a manufacturing trade but to a performing trade, which implies that not just repetitive skills are involved in the simile, but the apparent skill of a bard to read the nature of his audience, and to perform as they most need or want to hear, not to mention his skill at tuning and playing his instrument. Moreover this simile is not an isolated phenomenon; it fits in well with what could justly be called an ideological position that is already well established by the poet presiding over the poem, namely that poets deserve special recognition for their special cultural services to mankind.[5] This passage amounts to a claim on the poet's part that the poem is in some sense his private property, that he expects rewards and recognition for it, and not only that but especially recognition that his art makes him socially necessary as the one true guarantor of cultural permanence, for any hero or his tale. And, per corollary, it contains the insinuation that this poem, unlike other epic poems, perhaps unlike the actual *Iliad,* will be made to bear the indelible marks of a self-conscious artist's personal existence and individual gifts of creativity.

From even this brief analysis of certain crucial passages of the poem, a major point about the poem's plan or agenda arises for our consideration with respect to the poet's determination that his voice be heard and recognized as different from any and all other epic voices, whether of the *Iliad* or all other military epics. The novel and distinguishing marks of his individual voice appear in three crucial areas: 1) the personal area of prestige, a new-found pride and artistic self-regard, which he is proud enough to flaunt, as noted just now; 2) flowing from a sense of artistic control and dominance over the sequence, pace, and selection of materials to the point that the poet can both make the story do his individual bidding and make the reader see that this is happening, so that one praises him more—indeed the narrative element sometimes disappears almost completely, as in the simile just quoted, and the poet bare-handedly interferes to editorialize on behalf of himself, his trade, or his private ideas; and finally 3) a new sensation of his own ability to judge and criticize the assumptions—cosmic, social, and moral—that underlie the standard epic traditions from which his raw materials have come.

The Homeric Question has always revolved about precise and often technical questions of language and verse in Homer or about Homer's value as witness to the historical actualities of any given period of time, whether his own or that of the heroic age behind him. But these questions cover only a short range of all the data that the Homeric poems yield for one's curiosity to consider. The first three chapters discussed peycho-social matters that were manifestly present in the text. Likewise, the overall record of the poem contains evidence of authorial vanity, of the poet's interference in the development of the story, and of his desire for recognition. These two matters are also found in the data the poem gives the reader to study. As Cicero once asked rhetorically, why does one suppose Phidias carved a likeness of his own face in a corner of the shield held by his great statue of Athena—because the Athenian authorities who commissioned the work refused to let him sign his name to it,[6] and his vanity was determined to find a way to signify that it was his work. The poet of the *Odyssey* probably had no idea how he might sign his own work—that concept was probably unknown at his time—but I would argue that he clearly experienced a sense of repressed anonymity such as that of Phidias, not for bureau-cratic reasons that afflicted the latter, but because of the traditional nature of oral epic poetry, and the anonymity of its poet, with both of which he was far from content.

By deliberately repudiating the straightforward linear devel-opment of events in their natural order for the first eight books, the poet of the *Odyssey* was simultaneously defying tradition as represented by the *Iliad,* trying to gain admiration for his skill, and, perhaps as well, trying to throw potential imitators off their stride and into confusion should any of them attempt to perform his poem for themselves (as noted earlier, the order of books in the *Odyssey*—which is quite different from the order of the events—is extremely difficult to keep straight except after long familiarity, at least for literate audiences who deal with its written form, and I can find no evidence in the work of Parry and Lord that modern Serbian singers can handle poems that so contort the natural sequence of events[7]). Then too, in the second half of the poem, though the events are told in natural chronological order, the behavior of the main characters makes little sense unless one can refer not just to their experiences in the first half of the poem, but to the cunningly contrived manner of their telling. Neither Odysseus' reticence and caution, nor Penelope's impatience and desperation, for instance, would impress one as much as they do, I suspect, if the first half of the poem had been told in simple, linear fashion, without the contrivance of having Odysseus tell his adventures in books 9–11 at the end of his journeyings, so that he is carried back in memory to those first three years of the Wanderings when his fear and suspicions were still mounting rather than receding, as they logically should be doing now that he has nearly reached home, and just as Hermes and Calypso and Ino and the Phaeacians have assured him he will.

When Odysseus asks himself his poetic question at the beginning of book 9, he is saying—or rather the poet is making him say—that telling a good tale is a matter of strategic choices, and not simply the recounting of natural events. The mental processes by which this literary fact was discovered and then articulated here with admirable cunning on the poet's part are more astounding than critics of the poem have seemed to realize, for implied in this discovery are several other prior discoveries and discriminations, which should be enough to revolutionize the reader's view of the *Odyssey*. Among these other discoveries, at a minimum, there must have been the following : first, that the existence of a variety of poetic choices or strategies from which to choose implies that these different strategies do in fact already exist, and a poet is free to choose among them, plus the intuition that given poets can and will choose differently, and that one and the same poet may choose differently at different times; second, the existence of a variety of choices implies the ability of a poet to perceive a variety of needs and desires in himself or his audience, or a variety of poetic raw materials, which are the only three conceivable sources of a poet's desire to have a free choice of strategies in the first place; third and most important, there had to be the realization that the existence of a variety of strategies to choose from implies that a different strategy applied to the same materials would produce a very different sort of work, and that such a result would be another artifact, a different work of human creation, independent from that work which the author has in fact chosen to create.

These points are terribly important, especially the third. The first two reflect mainly on the nature and status of the artist as an independent being with power of the will to choose among a variety of strategies, and for reasons and purposes that he can foresee at the outset before he begins to perform or create. The third discovery reflects more on the nature of poetry itself, and it says something crucial and distinctive about how poetry was viewed by at least one poet who had a hand in fashioning our version of the *Odyssey,* for it implies that poems, in his view, are not social continuities, nor continuing traditions, nor things held in keeping by Muses. No, they are very different, and each one could conceivably be different from every other one, even if the subject matter remained essentially the same, depending on the strategies chosen and the aims the prevailing theory of oral epic has offered us about the conditions under which Greek heroic poetry was fabricated. It is clear from Albert Lord's *Singer of Tales,* that one thing the theory can not and will not tolerate is a suggestion that any given singer can make a significant number of moves in his single generation to affect the texture of the poem radically; that no one poet can lend a poem his own definitive stamp by the limited number of optional changes he can make in the received material.[8] I can not myself say whether or not the *Odyssey* successfully passes the Parry test for oral authorship—the lack of similes, except at odd or crucial places, seems to tell against it—but I can say that the *Odyssey* contains sufficient comment on poets and poetics that seems to point in quite a different direction, like the opening of the tale of the Adventures in book 9. True, that was but one line of text, and all the samples I used previously, or will use, are relatively short, but they are so different from anything found in the *Iliad* and so pregnant in themselves with meanings that differentiate the *Odyssey* both from the *Iliad* and from what modern theories about epic composition say about Greek epics, that it has seemed entirely justifiable to push their interpretation to the full. The *Odyssey* contains within itself notions of poetry and authorship that are deeply in conflict with both the *Iliad* and with modern theories about epic composition.

As far as one can tell from the *Iliad,* for a poet to sing "The Wrath of Achilles" (probably the real "title" of the *Iliad*) is for him to sing of a given account of a major heroic event that is felt to be the authoritative telling. Asked to sing his story again, the oral bard would sing virtually the same series of verses again, and though he would no doubt unconsciously alter many individual verses in small ways, and perhaps even forget or transpose minor episodes, his second version would still appear as a good extemporaneous paraphrase of the first. The oral bard suffers no temptation to sit down and consciously improve the song by meddling with the overt details, no conscious wish to rearrange, suppress, or doctor specific scenes or episodes for any sort of editorial purpose or rhetorical effect, partly because he has no thought of improving upon a tradition, and partly because, in a sense, the song is the self-possessing event : the poet can not own it, and thus can not make his own, conscious changes in it. In the case of the *Iliad,* the Muse guarantees that there is only one "Wrath of Achilles," and that the song and the events it recounts are a symbolic pair, and each is the other's support and vouchsafe of credibility and fidelity.* Odysseus' remark about poetic strategies, as well as other remarks about poets and poetry, whether already cited or to be noted below, conjure

* Could it be that Odysseus' reputation as a liar, and the poet's need to create several lies for him to tell in the course of the poem, moved one particular poet to realize that a tradition can be improved upon, for willful reasons, and thus to discover the idea, through prevarication perceived as an art form, of authorship and literature as a personally conceived fiction?

up a different view of what narrative song is. His words, at their simplest interpretation, point to the fact that the poem up to this point has been told backward, a virtuoso performance if nothing more, though I have argued in the first chapter that the purpose of this ordering is much more complex. But his words also insinuate the notion that poetry is only a means of telling a tale and that the means are subject to all sorts of variation depending upon a human poet's decisions, which in turn implies that to him poets are or ought to be individuals, taking pride in their individual creations and expecting to gain recognition for their creation, which would only be possible if poems were capable of being identified as the work of an individual and were free of major modification by a continuous bardic tradition.

This new, or at least different, conception of what poetry does and how it does it, is not inharmonious with much of the content of the *Odyssey*, as I have analyzed it, for just as the *Odyssey* begins with the statement of Zeus that men are mostly responsible for the moral events in their lives and must pay the penalty of their transgressions, so one may say that the poem also endeavors to claim that a poet is artistically and personally responsible for most of what happens in his tale. This marks it as his, and he is thereby entitled to personal pride in problems solved, and something approaching personal recognition for work well done. Moreover, just as the lower orders of society begin to raise their heads in *Odyssey*—Eumaeus, the old mill-woman, slaves, and even a dog!—and to claim, if not social justice, at least a recognition of the moral importance and seriousness of their wants, ideas, and sufferings, so too the bard begins to raise his head as well and to claim, if not a material gain for his poem, at least individual credit, prestige, and admiration for the personal achievements and qualities of his work. None of this could very likely have taken place at all, unless and until it was somehow discovered that a poem was not a continuing, traditional tale, something existing in the public domain and to which no one individual could lay claim, like the

Iliad, but an artifact, an object which, once fashioned, remained in the shape in which its artisan formed it, with which neither forgers nor other artisans could meddle without destroying its very fabric, which is part of the point Cicero was trying to make with his story about Phidias. Eternal realities, like the notion of a "Wrath," recorded in a perpetual poem, are not the sort of vehicle that can convey new and argumentative social ideas. They are not amenable to that much editorial comment and change in any given generation, and indeed they do not permit their poets to look upon them as property sufficiently private to encourage editorial changes for *any* purpose, social or otherwise.

The discoveries of the nature of individual art, which are implicit in Odysseus becoming a poet in book 9, must soon have led one or more poets to seek for means of making a poem still more individual and private. I have suggested just above that one or more poets discovered certain ways of looking at the practice of poetry and the dissemination of narrative tales that led to the understanding that a poem can be an individual artifact, which gives honor to its creator and which cannot be changed by others or be submerged into an anonymous tradition. But, that point having been reached, it must then have dawned on him or them that a poem can also be used, not just to tell its ostensible tale, but to advertize for the existence of crafty poets and to propagandize for their status and merits : to plead for applause for their better devices, and, finally, to bid for something like official status as poets owning personal literary property.

It is tempting to search for reasons explaining the differences between the self-effacing oral bard of a poem like the *Iliad* and the far more self-conscious, authorial personality of the poet of the *Odyssey* at play among its lines, by looking for a change in society between the times the two poems were gathered into more or less the shape they have today. Yet that temptation shall and should be resisted : we know so very little about the social conditions of the times in which the oral bards could have been working, and we can be sure that the social conditions portrayed in the *Iliad* are not those actually witnessed by the living poet—a point even good scholars tend to get confused about at times—that it would be a problem in all unknowns to begin to try sorting out all the possible variants of poetic conditions, social development, and political change. Homer, the poet of the *Iliad*, himself tells us that the heroic age had drawn to a close long before his day—he occasionally mentions a feat of daring or strength performed by one of his heroes that would be beyond men—*hoioi nun brotoi easi*—as they now exist, that is, in his own day. The poet of the *Iliad* is simply telling a tale of great heroes and kings, seen from a great distance, and perhaps a fading perspective (the tendency of typical epics to end with valedictories, as mentioned earlier). That these heroes and kings were claimed as ancestors by the ruling oligarchy of Homer's day is more than likely, and Homer no doubt earned a fair amount of his living singing for audiences of such persons, but it is notable that neither Homer nor his audiences knew how the arts and institutions of heroic society worked, from chariots to monarchy, either through personal experience or recorded memory, and therefore one must assume that the social and political conditions under which he operated were considerably different from those which may have obtained in the age of heroes, if the latter could be known, either now or then, which unfortunately they mostly cannot. Except for negative evidence of this sort, therefore, we have very little solid grounds for guessing how Homer's society operated, either, and still less for deciding whether his picture of heroic society is much more than a tradition and a dream.

Coming then to the *Odyssey* there is little more, I suspect, that one can do to obtain a clear picture of prevalent social usages, in order to see if the poet is either a harbinger of social change or a prophet threatening a society that has not changed enough to suit him. One can of course say at least that the poet of the *Odyssey* has little knowledge of the society of the heroic world, except that which he can guess from poems like the *Iliad,* and that he dislikes what he finds there. But this is not a very profitable field for speculation. Far better is to prospect in the areas of artistic competition and audience psychology. Whatever else the frequent intrusion of poets, poetry, and poetic problems into the poem may prove, it appears it must prove that the taste of audiences had shifted from that which found the anonymous oral bard telling his tales in a linear fashion totally satisfying. Obviously a new taste for complexity, social conundrums, peasant morality, and poetic illusionism had developed. One might add a new taste in word play—the "No Man" situation spoken of in chapter 1—quasi-comic exaggeration, and dubious situations in which both identity and morality are unclear. And, finally, to give Samuel Butler and Robert Graves their due, there was developing, apparently, a new taste for seeing females play a far larger part in literature. This seems to have coincided with the appearance of a poet of some genius and certainly great energy and inventiveness who was more than eager to lend himself—or herself—to these new trends because they suited his own clamorous insistence upon the social worth of poets and their rights to recognition that they had not previously enjoyed.

It is simply a matter of fact that the poet in the *Odyssey* has a changed set of attitudes toward his work, different from those evident in the *Iliad*. Why this happened is probably less important than the fact that it happened, at least insofar as the further history of literature is concerned. Very little is gained by speculating whether the poet of the *Odyssey* was rankled by more than the anonymity of the oral bard, or to assume that he had resolved, in a period of social change, to make his bid for glory and recognition out of some deeply felt need either to second the social change he saw going on about him, or to provoke social change that he wanted to see continue. Either would be a thesis no better than a hundred others.

The facts are, however, that the poet of the *Odyssey* did change the relationship between author and poem, for whatever reasons, and the changes he wrought are almost unimaginably significant, whatever may have led to them in any subjective sense. I myself lean toward the view that the poet's motives were largely artistic; that is, that he found the world of oral poetry old and stifling, yet being emulous and ambitious as Kirk has guessed, he wanted to outdo poems like the *Iliad* but mainly by being as different as possible in his treatment of what had once been traditional material. I myself think that this poet wanted to dismantle Homer on all fronts: to dissolve and even ridicule the Homeric portrait of the hero, by conducting the one reputed heroic survivor into the new era by purging him of all heroic characteristics just to permit him to survive; to deride and subvert the authority of a Homer or an *Iliad* on heroic virtues and life choices—for example, the speech of Achilles' ghost, which derides of the first premise of the *Iliad;* and finally to attack and outreach the poet of the *Iliad* himself, both by creating a far more individualistic and quirky poem and by injecting the persona of the poet into the poem in ways that Homer would never have dreamed. The occasional polemics against and contradictions of Homer to be found in the *Odyssey* would indeed agree with other points that are observed in this book. The *Odyssey* seems designed to oppose—to oppose a revered conception of the heroic life, of course, but also to oppose a presentation of heroic life, a natural epic like the *Iliad* perhaps, a poem which demands that its audience accept the heroic view of human worth and moral values. That may just be naive on the part of the *Iliad;* the *Iliad* may not be trying to make a moral point at all—but it is a challenge to the *Odyssey* and at least one of its poets, and the *Odyssey* moves vigorously to contradict and sabotage as much as it can lay its hands on of the heroic program of virtues and moral worth. The *Odyssey* exists in the shadow of another view of the heroic, and another great and grandiose poem, most probably the *Iliad,* but perhaps some or many others; very little of its subtler maneuvers make any sense except when viewed as challenges and contradictions hurld at a preexisting poem, a poem that entirely refuses to question the greatness and worthiness of the old heroes and their code. But, at the same time, the *Odyssey* makes very little more sense unless one sees it as a challenge on the artistic level as well: it has both an enemy and a rival and both are probably the *Iliad*. It is almost obvious that artistic dissatisfaction, emulation, and pride are enormously important motives behind the poem's composition. Judging solely by the evident facts, one could view the priorities either way: it may well be that the cart moves resolutely before the horse, and that the determination of the poet to outshine the *Iliad* was a resolve taken prior to any ideological or principled decision to attack the social assumptions of the *Iliad*.

What is certain, however, is that at least one poet involved in a major way with the composition of the poem as it now stands was concerned with attacking the image of heroic greatness such as that found in the *Iliad*, as well as injecting into it a role for poets to play, both his own role and that of the poets he writes about. (The thought occurs to ask whether, on the assumptions of the Parry-Lord school, it is likely that laudatory verse passages *about poets* performing were part of the materials an oral poet would find in his tradition? Somehow, that seems the most unlikeliest thing in the world.) Finally, one must consider whether or not the various gestures made by the *Odyssey* toward a revaluation of the heroic era may not be the natural result of the passage of time, during which old materials and old ideas have simply worn out. It is rather general in fact for national literatures to follow cycles that begin typically with naive primary epic whose central characters are kings and fighting chiefs, and then as the cycle unfolds, for the concern of literature to move outward and downward from the center of society and a concern with its rulers, to find more interesting characters and themes in lesser classes and in purely private persons, then in inferior castes, until, finally, at the end of a cycle when society is urban, cynical, and jaded, to turn to the sick, the crazed, and the criminal as the only vehicles that can still generate useful literary inspiration. One must not neglect to consider whether the social differences between *Iliad* and

Odyssey are not due mainly to the fact that this process is already beginning in Greek literary consciousness. In chapter 2 it was noted that either Odysseus or the reader is forced to confront all sorts of persons from lower social stations and to interest himself in their thoughts—even the emotions of a dog are subject to study! These episodes are interesting in themselves, besides whatever they contribute to the story of Odysseus, or at least the poet thought so, and in using them he has affixed a very different tone to the poem from anything in the *Iliad,* since they lead attention away from the social center, and one wonders if there is not a touch of inevitability in all that. Perhaps great heroes and purely military doings can be honestly and honorably celebrated only once in each national literature.

The role of the poet in the *Odyssey* is strange, puzzling, perhaps unique. I can think of no other sort of work showing quite the same odd willfullness in the way the author handles his story, except a much later genre, Attic Old Comedy, where the author, by convention, steps in and out of his work, meddling, declaiming, accusing, and always trying to tilt reactions in favor of what he wants one to think about his tale. The net effect is a strong impression of authorial presence in the poem, as though he were at the reader's elbow, nudging him to see the point he had in mind with this or that passage, word, or event.

It has been noticed, perhaps almost from the beginning, that the appearance of two poets as characters in the *Odyssey* has something to tell about the poet who established the poem. They are of course only minor characters in the overall tale, but at least when they are onstage, they are near its center, and a good deal of attention is invested in their skills and their predicaments. What their presence has to tell, however, is open to varied interpretation. Phemius, the journeyman poet on Ithaca, and Demodocus, the grand master on Scheria, were once naively taken as self-evidentiary portraits, perhaps self-portraits in the literal sense, of the ancient bard—the ancient legend of the blind Homer owes literally all but a tiny fraction of its origin to the portrait of the blind Demodocus[9]—as well as descriptions of the bard's procedures and social position. It is, moreover, safe, and easy, to conclude that the sketches of these poets contain a fair amount of self-promotion by the poet who created them, as propaganda for the standing of his craft and its title to emoluments commensurate with its skills and social value to other men. By having Odysseus first offer Demodocus some choice cuts of meat from his own platter in book 8, and then later proclaim his worthiness of such favorable treatment, one may safely say, the poet responsible for this passage was doing a little genteel advertising for himself and his profession. Likewise, when the fate of the honest Phemius is decided favorably, the reader is also witnessing a certain degree of melodrama engineered by the poet responsible for the scene, asking sympathy for the fact that bards are often undeservedly subject to harsh or contumacious treatment by other men better placed and more powerful than they, as well as to dangers and threats that they deserve even less. The dignities and security of Demodocus may represent the ideal; the precarious position of Phemius may be closer to the real picture of the poet's position in society. There is indeed something almost gothic in the way Phemius is first abused by the Suitors, then constrained to entertain them, then almost hanged by Odysseus for doing what he had no choice but to do if he were to save his life and livelihood.

But, beyond these rather easy-to-make observations, there is a good deal more to the appearance of Phemius and Demodocus in the *Odyssey*. The songs sung by the two poets are for the most part epic—the *Iliad* or epics like it, and they are referred to only in summary fashion, not quoted. But Demodocus' song about Ares and Aphrodite is quoted, and it strikes me more as a sort of prize song, more familiar from the medieval tradition of the Meistersinger than oral epic. It is a set piece, a nugget of high polish, which a poet, who might normally engage mainly in the recitation of oral epic verse, has prepared for a special occasion; and as such it is his special creation, compared with the more general run of his songs—which are seemingly traditional, which is why, surely, they are not quoted! The fact that this song of Demodocus is related in great detail appears to be a clue to its difference in status. One wonders, therefore, if the situation the *Odyssey* portrays with respect to poets does not resemble more closely the medieval tradition in which known bards with real names made their living by both reciting the great traditional epics and creating their own poems on special occasions. In other words, in the *Odyssey* itself do we not begin to see the poet moving from behind his mask of anonymity, and taking up the practice of individual composition when not engaged in reciting traditional tales; do we not see here evidence of the existence of poems in which the poet's personal contribution to the result rises greatly in expectation of personal awards? Even if the songs of Phemius were forced out of him by the twin imperatives of fear for his skin and a desire to eat, and thus may not count for much, the songs of Demodocus bear very close inspection. Demodocus, while he can sing epic verse with great skill and feeling—enough to bring tears to the stranger's eyes—when he first is called upon to entertain the guests assembled by King Alcinous to entertain their anonymous guest at a feast, he tells not some epic tale but the rowdy tale of the amour of Ares and Aphrodite. The point of the tale is to lift spirits and instill general good will with a tale that is essentially comic, crude, and has a bit of suspense added in. On this occasion, there is no mention of a Muse or any invocation at all. The tale is simply told—and retold in our poem, mostly by indirect narration except for direct quotations of speeches among the gods—and in great detail, unlike the epic songs of Demodocus which come later and are only summarized, with no quotations at all. Demodocus, then, so far as the *Odyssey* tells it, owns this poem and owes it to no one or nothing. It is his property, owed neither to a Muse nor a tradition nor anything but his own genius and skill and sense of humor.

Our poet, of course, has created this poem for Demodocus to narrate, and perhaps the very clever will see even here the beginning of our poet's campaign for recognition as a creative artist and independent craftsman, free of undue subjection to traditions, Muses, or social notions about his inferior status, though still only in book 8 and anticipating book 9, where the more startling claims observed above are made.

Beyond all that, other things about Demodocus' poem engage interest. First, there is the simple fact that this is not a heroic tale at all, but a bit of gossip about Olympus, with none of the stateliness or urgency of passages in the *Iliad* that repeat divine scandals of any sort. Such passages, moreover, are always directly applied to the mapor theme of the poem in the *Iliad,* and are never left for one to guess at their literary point. Thus the possibility broached in chapter 2, that this tale, though meant as innocuous entertainment by Demodocus, may in fact have serious thematic overtones for the hero Odysseus, given his by-now pathological suspicions about everything under the sun, is clearly not so obvious that it requires no explanation at all, and is indeed an interpretation, not a self-evident gloss on the text, as cameo-tales are in the *Iliad.* Odysseus, I believe, is forced to hear this tale by design, such that it works on his fears that his return to Ithaca will resemble all too closely and uncomfortably this very tale of wifely infidelity and scheming revenge, with him in the role as the old and despised Hephaestus, and one or more of the Suitors cast as the brilliant, golden Ares. Thus, on my interpretation, the placement of the tale just here in book 8 is extremely ominous for Odysseus, and just right as a device to alert one to the complexities of the plot, as well as its excellence as a plot. Yet just as surely, none of this was intended by Demodocus, nor is it patently obvious to any reader, since no scholar has yet noticed it. If that is true, then the tale resembles not the story of Achilles singing of the glory of past heroes in his tent, but much more the Phoenix digression in the same book of the *Iliad.* Yet, if that is so, its differences with the Phoenix tale are more exciting and suggestive than the similarities. The double digression of the Phoenix reminiscences—his own stubbornness and the stubbornness of Meleager—has a rather obvious point in the development of the *Iliad,* which no one who is fully awake could really miss: stubbornness in the refusal of other men's offers of compromise can lead to nothing but grief for the stubborn man who clings to a too-exalted notion of his own honor and uniqueness. The tale of Demodocus, if it has the thematic significance seen in it, is far more subtle. It is not told directly to the man it may affect most closely, but to a general and routine social assemblage of which he is but one member, though an honored guest; nor is it told, apparently, with any specific knowledge of his present state of mind or feelings or fears; nor, finally is it provoked by any evidence in the narrative about Odysseus that might subliminally have suggested its pertinence to Demodocus. Thus, if the tale is more than pure entertainment, and has something to con-tribute to the major thematic movement of the poem along the lines suggested, then two significant advances have been made between the *Iliad* and the *Odyssey*. First, it is now thought possible to delineate the moral predicament of a character by means of a purely symbolic and juxtaposed reference, rather than by the more labored means of obvious similes or moral exempla deliberately aimed at one character by another, as in the Phoenix episode. And second, the agency for conveying this sort of information to an audience is now not a character earnestly involved with the hero on a personal basis, but a chance acquaintance, who, through art, rather than direct contact or involvement, manages to express something important about the hero's predicament, not because he really knows the hero's predicament in particular, but, because as an artist, he knows what predicaments can be in general! This new status of course makes the artist much more than the channel of a tradition. And it makes us recall once again Alcinous' praise of Odysseus himself as a tale-teller almost as good as a real bard : there the king expressed special reverence for knowledge on the bard's part; now, perhaps one can see what sort of knowledge he meant, not that of brute facts, but of how men generally act and how events plausibly unfold.

Finally, there is the song of the Sirens in book 12, not an overwhelming matter in itself, but an example of the poet seldom failing to seize a chance to "magnify his office," as Dr. Johnson says "it behooveth every man" to do. Whether readers of the Odyssey would agree that the song of the Sirens is really of unearthly quality, as the poet claims, it is noteworthy that the poet has been inspired to design the event so that he can try his hand at whatever he thinks unearthly poetry might be, by having Odysseus let himself listen to this music and thus be able to report it to his hearers on Phaeacia years later. (Where, interestingly, he, who is now a poet pro tem and recites this other poetry—a kind of double-mirror effect arranged, naturally by the poet!) Why Odysseus did not plug his own ears with wax, as he did with the rest of his crew, is hard to say, unless the poet wanted to stage yet another ambitious project that ultimately confers one more token of superiority and intelligence upon himself. Here, too, though the occasion is of slight importance in itself, I assume that the oral tradition would hardly have supplied any significant matter for a purely oral bard to work with, and therefore I suggest that this passage too represents essentially free and individual composition by a poet who has some sort of assurance that his creation would remain essentially his.[10]

The theory of oral poetry holds that the oral poet drew upon a remembered, though not memorized, stock of traditional materials in retelling an epic tale (emphasis on the retelling). These materials existed in great abundance and an accomplished singer could vary his treatment of successive episodes without boring repetitions. But there is no evidence to suggest that there existed as a part of this stock of traditional materials whole scenes in which bards themselves became characters in the fictions themselves, or told discrete tales whose only fictional purpose was to entertain other characters rather than to advance the plot or interact with those characters. Still less does the theory offer a hint that the preexistent stock of poetic materials included passages, from whole episodes to brief similes or lines, whose only evident purpose was to allow the poet to cry up his wares and advertise his profession in the very act of telling a tale, or to show off his own talent and cleverness as just that. Bards appear only once in the *Iliad* (book 24), in an anonymous group leading the mourning dirges for Hector, where they seem more like priests, in any case. There is no indication that the *Iliad* contains any such evidence of its or its poets' concern with the bard, his function, or his social status, and, as was noted above, the *Iliad* rather assumes that song itself exists outside the real control of particular bards, as something objective on the heroic landscape.

Some scholars have written as though the pictures of bardic activity in the *Odyssey* were in fact a record of the condition of the oral poet and his methods of operation, but that is only a guess, and is derived from only these passages in the *Odyssey*, where the evidence is most unlikely to prove the contention for which it is being used.[11] Also, in no incident of the *Odyssey* where poets appear and/or poetry comes up for notice, from the longest scene to the shortest simile, is the passage merely decorative or neutral—in all cases these are occasions apparently specially made up to praise poets and poetry—or to excuse them if they are forced to entertain the wicked—and to celebrate the poets' social worthiness and right to recognition. It is on the face of it extremely improbable that the long anonymous tradition of oral poetry, pure and simple, has manufactured passages such as these to be available for other bards to use in the course of telling the usual military epic; and thus find their way into the *Odyssey*.

From what has been learned about the oral bard's social status, it seems unlikely that any particular oral bard would have dreamed up such passages on his own—even granting his ability to do so in the abstract—because it would have been pretentious of him and might well have angered his patrons, were he to employ them, even if he could invent them. But, even if here and there a bard with a touch more personal vanity than the average were inspired to try to inject something into his poem to praise himself and his trade, the oral bard, knowing how poems circulated, from man to man and from generation to generation, would instantly have realized that the next man who picked up his song, with bits of self-advertisement clinging to it, even if he tried to reproduce these bits in all innocence, would get half of them wrong because of their unfamiliar tone, or would forget where to put them, since they would seldom in all probability have a natural an inevitable place in a standard epic tale. Or, even if a successor should have got them right, whose praise would he be uttering? His own, though unwittingly? That of their true author? That of all poets? No one could possibly tell. Would such a purpose sufficiently arouse an oral poet to take the trouble required to compose materials full of self-praise, with such unpromising prospects as to its likely impact with the public? I think not. The oral poet introduced by Parry and Lord, if he thought of glory at all, thought of the glory of a great performance—more like an actor than an author—and his reward was a rousing supper and perhaps a comfortable bed for a few days afterwards, not literary fame.

Even thus far, I think, there is enough evidence to suggest two things: that at least one poet who had a large part in constructing the *Odyssey* as it stands possessed a psychological stance very different from that of the hypothetical oral poet, and certainly very different from the poet of the *Iliad,* both with respect to his own function as a poet and the social status deriving therefrom. .And he had reason to believe, or thought he had reason to believe, that his control over his work was going to be different in kind, not just degree, from that of the oral bard or the poet of the *Iliad,* so that the poem would remain essentially his through time and therefore he could both logically and plausibly claim and exercise both the pride of authorship and its consequent proprietorship within the fabric of the poem itself. No other hypothesis, I would argue, so neatly explains the poet's complicated attempts to inject himself and his kind into the poem, not to mention hints that his craft is controlling the work and has turned it into a work of art, from being a mere report of nature, and that it is therefore inimitable.

The last point, inimitability, may or may not be provable by objective criteria, and so I have not made a great point of it, though I am not the first to hint that the construction of the Odyssey is phenomenally complicated and devious[12]—like its hero—and that this may be a hint of something different and perhaps unique in its composition. My reason for avoiding a full-dress discussion of this issue is based on two problems: one, it would simply take a disproportionate amount of space and time to go into all the details, and two, the same sort of argument, before the advent of the Parry thesis, used to be made about the composition of the *Iliad* by what are called *unitarians,* against the rival school of critics called *analysts.* What may or may not seem inimitable to any particular generation of scholars is not always a law of nature or anything like it to the next generation. My only reason for going even briefly into the question here at all is because my observations, unlike so many in past generations, have nothing to do with global concepts like genius or grandeur and the like. They concern lowly, more mechanical things. First, as noted in passing earlier, I have never met anyone, who after only a few readings of the *Odyssey* —unless warned beforehand what would be asked—could possibly give back the ordering of the books in anything approaching their correct sequence. In fact, the naive reader, no doubt like the naive hearer in antiquity, is quite quickly confused about the structure of the poem and about where particular events occur in it. In this the *Odyssey* stands in sharpest contrast to the *Iliad,* whose overall order and main events could be given back after one reading by a reasonably alert fourteen-year-old. Granted, the story of the *Iliad* can be opened and closed like an accordion, with the addition of exclusion of many episodes that could go anywhere or nowhere, like the *Doloneia* and the *Diomedeia,* but the essential story line, which is identical with the order of the poem, is very hard to forget, not hard to remember. Now the memory of the oral poet, I take it, though richer by far than that of the naive reader in detail and genre scenes and formulaic language, is essentially like that of the naive reader in this one respect: his memory, taxed as it is to provide circumstantial description and plausible speech for each successive episode in his tale, can not be simultaneously taxed to remember in what order the episodes occur in the first place. The natural temporal order of events, on all the evidence available, would be assumed as his starting point by the typical oral bard. Digressions may be admitted, but they would be simple digressions, like the tales of Phoenix or the story of Bellerophon in the *Iliad,* and not the almost conspiratorial intricacies of the *Odyssey.* (Professor Woodhouse's book on the composition of the *Odyssey* came out just a little too soon for him to comment on the Parry thesis of the oral poet, which was our bad luck, because Woodhouse saw the *Odyssey* as a massive reshuffling of what had once been a typical and straightforward heroic epic about the adventures of Odysseus returning home, redone to make room for some poet's sudden discovery of concern for Telemachus. Woodhouse apparently assumed that the poet was dealing either with a written text or at least a memorized text—he himself, if not his audience, must have been literate simply to engage in the textual checkers game Woodhouse assumes to have taken place. Had Woodhouse thought of the question of the poet's own artistic ambitions, set against a background of oral poetry, he was sufficiently close to reach a solution of the sort under discussion here; as it is, one gets from him only glancing blows of insight here and there on the question.)

As Lord has reported, the oral bards he and Parry interviewed in Serbia always regarded their songs as fixed and finished, though in fact they always varied them to some degree at each successive retelling. Paradoxically, to our minds, they also always assumed that there would be yet another telling and performance to give—at which time more unwitting changes would occur.[13] This sort of thing, I am prepared to accept, could very well account for the condition of the *Iliad,* whose main turning points are a perfectly natural ordering of events. But I cannot see how the *Odyssey* would survive the sort of memory control that the oral bard seems to possess, which is a command of *typical* detail, not that of an extremely complicated, perverse overall structure and detail, especially if it in any serious way runs counter to the natural chronological order of events. At some point, if one were to suppose the structure of the present *Odyssey* to have been the original form, the retelling of the tale, as it now stands, by successive generations of bards would have produced a fatal collapse of control and nothing but chaos as a result, which would have left no *Odyssey* at all. (Indeed it seems frivolous to entertain the idea that a poem constructed like the *Odyssey* could have been produced by the oral tradition in the first place, or have been the original, which was then left to be deranged and disordered per impossible by still later generations of bards.) No, there is no reason to suppose that it would ever have entered the head of an oral poet to build the *Odyssey* as it now is, setting himself pitfalls every step of the way in the first half of the poem. Much cleaner is the Woodhouse hypothesis that an original and unimaginative Odysseus epic, completely linear in structure, and probably beginning with the opening of the present book 9, had been developed as saga, as Woodhouse calls it, and that this traditional poem was taken up and overhauled by an individual poet of superior powers, and no small amount of gall, one might add, who willfully distorted it and turned it upside down to make an individualistic poem that suited a very personal ideology or whim. Whether or not Telemachus is the center of that whim may not be to the point any more, because the Parry thesis has suggested by indirection other grounds for this poet's willfulness than those Woodhouse imagined, but his overall observations on the construction of the *Odyssey* are still of unrefuted power.)

That something like authorial vanity, nay, even personal pride, may underlie much of the *Odyssey* must have struck some readers as improbable because the theory of oral poetry seems to rule out the idea that the anonymous oral bard possesses either the social station or the sense of control over his materials, which are in some sense public domain long before they reach him, to atempt to make his poem his own and attach to it any signs of individual control, much less of individual artistic vanity and pride. My response, especially in the pages immediately preceding, has been to argue that according to these notions of how the oral poet functions, the *Odyssey*, or at least its last or next-to-last poet, clearly functioned quite differently

The *Odyssey* quarrels with the idea of poetic anonymity in several ways. Most simply, it gives two poets not just roles as minor actors in the tale, but gives them names as well, when they might just as well have been called *bards, aoidi,* and been left at that. Moreover their names are "made-up" names; any Greek could tell instantly what they mean,* and that they are connected with their roles. *Phemius* means the *man of speech* and *Demodocus* means *received* or *honored by the people.* The latter, as the more important and statelier poet of the two, is the object of considerable attention by the poet as to how he practices his craft, and the descriptions offered by the poet fail to tally with either the role of the poet in the *Iliad* or with what the theory of oral poetry appears to tell. The main emphasis is upon Demodocus' knowledge and skill. Though both his memory and his Muse are also mentioned with praise, they do not play the same role they do in the *Iliad.* Demodocus' Muse is con-

---

* Most of the names in the *Iliad,* and thus in the oral tradition, are clearly pre-Greek and hence defy etymological analysis. This includes the names of the gods and most of the heroes (not Agamemnon or Menelaus; nor, on the Trojan side, Hector, Andromache, and Astyanax). Mainly it is minor characters like Protesilaus who have transparently Greek names —though some have transparently foreign names, too, like Phoenix and Bellerophon. The *Odyssey,* in contrast, abounds in Greek etymological names, from Calypso to Anticleia, and from Cyclops to Alcinous, Antinous and Theoclymenos. In fact, wherever the tradition appears to be vague or silent, the poet of the *Odyssey* leaps to invent a name with great relish, as he may have done with the name of Odysseus' grandfather Autolycus, "Lone Wolf." Indeed, the poet even essays an etymology for the name of Odysseus, deriving it from the verb *odyssasthai, to cause trouble,* in the famous flashback scene triggered by the discovery of his scar in book 19.

gratulated for teaching him poetic craft in general, or for occasionally suggesting a theme, but it is nowhere implied that his Muse sings the song through him, for then it would be idle to praise his knowledge.[14] This seems to imply that an intellectual factor has newly been recognized as playing a part in poetic composition, a factor that makes judgments and choices, at least for sorting out received stories in order to tell the best ones, or the best versions of them. Indeed, in the case of the ribald tale of Ares and Aphrodite, no Muse is even hinted at as the source of the tale, in any sense, whether of prior training, or of suggestion, much less of doing the singing through a poet vehicle. It is moreover implied that the skillful poet has true knowledge of the real world, not just of an oral tradition, which allows him to tell a convincing tale—otherwise Alcinous' praise of Odysseus for having knowledge like a bard, would not make a great deal of sense. The episode with Demodocus indicates that the concept of a poet's function has considerably expanded since the *Iliad,* in the direction of crediting the poet with greater freedom of choice, greater knowledge and responsibility, and a greater claim to credit for the artistic quality of his finished songs. He is less and less like an agent of a divinity, still less like the priest or the seer, with whom he could not begin even to compete in the *Iliad.*

The *Odyssey* is not of course a signed work of literature —unless perchance the poet was actually named Demodocus or Phemius. One might argue that a signature should be the acid test for granting the *Odyssey* the status of an individual work of art. But, may I say that it may well be signed, though no one has noticed it.

The first signed work of letters in the history of western civilization, one normally thinks, is the *Theogony* of the Boeotian poet Hesiod, writing perhaps in the last quarter of the eighth century B.C. Hesiod's poem opens with a description, rather than a pure invocation, of the Pierian Muses, first as they danced on Mount Helicon, and then went forth into the world at night praising the gods, who are then listed by Hesiod. At line 22 of the poem, Hesiod finally juxtaposes the Muses and himself:

And one day they taught Hesiod beautiful song as he shepherded his flocks under holy Helicon.[15]

Hesiod's procedure here is illuminating on the question of literary property, as the concept first began to dawn at the beginning of our letters. Basically, Hesiod wants to do two things simultaneously, to gain authority for his poem and its doctrines, which he does by associating himself and his poetry with the Muses, but in his case, as he is writing didactic poetry, he must try to keep his poem his own and tamperproof, because lessons and preachments, unlike stories, would naturally suffer unacceptable deformation in being carried down the ages by oral bards.[16] (Before the invention of printing, the major danger authors feared for their works was interpolation, not plagiarism.) It is also notable that Hesiod makes his encounter with the Muses an accidental occurrence—he was about his own mundane business tending flocks when they encountered him—and he limits it to a single occasion during which the Muses taught him song not *a* song or *this* song, but song in general, the overall capacity to sing for the public and to do them good by singing. Indeed, he nowhere says that the Muses taught him the *Theogony* or any particular song; though when he met them they had just previously been singing about the race of the gods, he does not say he heard it, or that his song is their song. Moreover, he says they taught him, in the past not the present. He is no longer in any sort of direct contact with them. In fact, he observes a little later ((lines 31–32) that, at most, they taught him his subject matter.

They breathed into me divine speech, so that I could celebrate what has gone before, as well as what will be.

Theogony makes no prophecies that one can detect, and tells only what has been, while a later poem of Hesiod, *Works and Days,* in certain places tells what will be. *Theogony* then tells only a part of what the Muses taught Hesiod, and the teaching is mainly about cosmic reality, to a degree about the method of recording and rehearsing it, and not at all, on Hesiod's telling, about the words or phrases to be used for the task. Then they (lines 33–34):

> . . . ordered me to hymn the origin of the everlasting ones, and themselves from first to last.

He is ordered to sing, having been taught a skill—he has not been taught a specific song. Moreover, the Muses had told him (lines 26–28)

> Shepherds of the desert, shamefaced wretches, mere bellies, we know how to say many lies which look like truth, but when we wish we can pronounce the truth as well.

These words have frequently been taken as a slur in Homer's direction, and it is safe enough to say that they are a slur in the direction of some epic poem that took the Muses for its authority, and against which Hesiod seems to be declaring some sort of literary war. This last fact is particularly important, for it indicates that strong bias, a rage to set a record straight, may well be the factor that began the tradition of composing scratchily individual and contentious literary works at the outset of the tradition. This, as much as Hesiod's signature, makes it clear that his *Theogony* is a case of personal, private authorship, literature in the sense that one naturally understands and assumes it to be, as a private expression and a private possession, a vehicle for a single man's views, passions, judgments, and even his quirks.

Now there is an interesting progression as among *Theogony,* the *Iliad* and the *Odyssey* on the self-expression of their respective authors. And it is a clue, to be taken into consideration with all the others advanced in this chapter, as to the literary status of the poem. Whereas on the one hand the poet of the *Iliad* makes no reference to himself at the beginning of the poem, while Hesiod, on the other hand, boldly signs his name to *Theogony,* the poet of the *Odyssey* does something that falls halfway between the two; he places the personal pronoun *moi,* "me" in the first line of his poem, and indeed just after its first word *andra,* "man." "Sing to me of the man. . . ." Or perhaps more exactly: "relate the man to me," the verb in this case being a rare and odd one, *ennepe,* which seems actually to mean *track down* or *search out,* a significant verb for a wandering hero, perhaps. Now by juxtaposing the pronoun indicating his own personality with the noun meaning Odysseus, the poet has succeeded in making his personality confront that of his hero, and perhaps is even trying to blend them as he seems to in other places. Moreover, the first line was apparently crucial as the ordinary way in which poems were "named" for reference purposes in earlier antiquity.

The titles *Iliad* and *Odyssey* for the two Greek epic poems have no documentary support earlier than Herodotus.[17] While the usage could well be earlier than Herodotus, it probably cannot be much earlier, and it is my speculation that the coining of titles for Homer's two epics has something to do with the influence of Athenian tragic dramas, which appear to be the first literary works in history to bear anything like a title that is not a part of the body of the literary text itself. (The familiar titles of Hesiod's poems are descriptive of the content of his poems, but they look like a librarian's descriptions, especially *Works and Days*; it is extremely unlikely that they can be attributed to Hesiod himself.)[18] Even the early tragedies, one may guess, were entitled mainly to give interested parties, like judges and the Athenian public at the dramatic festivals, a rough method of quick reference—it would seem they could be quite casual, and may have been coined by the public or the judges rather than the author. The titles of many tragedies that name their choruses, like Aeschylus' *Eumenides* or Euripides' *Phoenician Women,* in themselves give no clue to their subjects, and well may have attached to the plays, not by their authors, but by an audience or by bureaucrats impressed, for some reason, especially by the choruses. Thus, for a very long time, even after titles became at least marginally useful, they do not seem to have been thought of much importance. In the prose genres, too, titling seems to have held very little importance for authors, or readers; prose essays like those in the Hippocratic corpus, or the essays, in prose or verse, of the Pre-Socratics seem to have had to make do with simple, barely descriptive titles, like "On Nature." Plato's dialogues are titled from the name of their narrator, like the *Phaedo,* or from the principal character, not counting Socrates, like the *Protagoras,* but these, too, may not be original with their author. Thus *Iliad* and *Odyssey* are late, off-hand, and not very significant titles for the works ascribed to Homer.

So how, then, before titles came into use at all, did an author expect others to be able to name or refer to his work? A glance at the historians gives us a clue. The first sentences of Herodotus and Thucydides are, respectively: "This is the research of Herodotus of Halicarnassus. . . ," and, "Thucydides the Athenian has composed. . . ." Gomme, in his commentary on the latter, notes that Thucydides' first sentence is the title page as it were of the historian's work, and was clearly meant to follow Herodotus as a model.[19] (Gomme notes, further, that Xenophon does not follow this practice in either his *Hellenica* nor the *Anabasis,* and indeed it may be that Xenophon is the first Greek author to give much thought to titles, and to use suggestive or abstract words for titles, as the two works just named may indicate, as well as some of his other titles, like *Cyropaedia* or *Memorabilia.*) If Thucydides is following Herodotus, whom is Herodotus following? Though Herodotus himself is our source of the titles *Iliad* and *Odyssey,* it would seem that his writer's instinct led him to introduce his own work not with an abstraction such as *Iliad* or *Odyssey,* but in such a way that it appears as his, perhaps more clearly than if he had an abstract title, as Xenophon would do two generations later. By putting his name in the title sentence, Herodotus is marking the work as his own, as best he could manage it. What instinct prompted this? Herodotus, called by Longinus, "the most Homeric of men," was quite obviously steeped in Homer, and for his day and in prose, he had acquired a quasi-Homeric knack for continuous narration. He probably followed "Homer" in this instance, too, and the poem he had to guide him was—because it had to be—the *Odyssey*, not the *Iliad*, which has no indication in its first line of authorship at all. The *Odyssey* does. The difficulty here is not that Homer of the *Iliad* could hardly be the Homer of the *Odyssey*. Herodotus, on the other hand, could not have known that, and for him Homer was the author of both *Iliad* and *Odyssey*. It seems clear that the *Odyssey* suggested to him how to entitle and sign his work as best he could.

Though it is small and brief, that supposedly simple pronoun "me," *moi,* sitting in the second place in the first line of the *Odyssey,* has tremendous force. For Herodotus, who would have assumed that the *Odyssey* was a written work, because he had never heard of oral poets, the traditional name Homer was as real a literary reality as the name Hesiod—or Herodotus. Or perhaps even more real, because Herodotus would have assumed that the author of the *Odyssey* could count on every one knowing his name, and therefore of having no need to inject more than the simple pronoun into his first line, the crucial line of the text for literary identification, and that by which the work would in fact be known to posterity.

The importance of first lines, then, is indicated by evidence running in two directions. Looking back toward an earlier day, prose writers indicate that to assure their property rights to their own works, it was necessary to sign their texts as early as possible in their works. Looking forward from the day of unsigned poetic literature, writers (or composers, however they composed) saw no way to insure the identification of their works as their own but to put into their first lines some indication of their personality, or some other mark of their individuality. Clearly, for the first four or five centuries of Greek literature, writers expected to be cited and recollected by the quotation of their key first lines, which could either be made memorable in themselves (tragic first lines, especially those of Euripides, as in *Medea, Bacchae,* or *Hippolytus*) or could be fashioned to contain a sufficiently clear reference to the author as to make his proprietary interest in the work hard to ignore. Thus, given all the possible conditions under which literature could have been produced—epic, personal lyric, choral lyric celebrating victorious athletes and produced for payment, and even drama—it appears that the best way to fix a seal of ownership on one's work was to make the first line eminently quotable, or to inject oneself into it, or to do both simultaneously. The poet of the *Odyssey* seems not to have imagined how he could inject his name into his epic, an impossibility in any case, given the nature of the epic, but he seems to have done the next best thing, by putting the pronoun "me" into the first line, and in the next most honored position, following the word *andra,* "man," meaning Odysseus. The two words in order tell the story, I suggest, of the two most importnat things the poet can conceive, the hero himself and the poet who tells his story. It is quite clear that the only convenient way of referring to the poem one calls an *Odyssey,* in the centuries before Herodotus or some other fifth-century Athenian most likely coined the terms *Iliad* and *Odyssey,* would have been to quote its first line, or more likely, its first half-line, *Andra moi ennepe Mousa.* This practice, I suspect, was already well established at a very early date, and it seems no risky speculation to guess that the poet of the *Odyssey* knew the *Iliad* by its first half-line, *Mēnin aeide the*a, "Sing, O goddess, the wrath." (The title *Iliad* would have struck both the poet of the *Odyssey* and the many poets of the *Iliad* as a blunder, I suspect : the programmatic first line of the poem itself makes a much better title, and this fact was acknowledged in practice even by literate poets throughout antiquity though they frequently signed their works in the modern fashion, for their titles pale in comparison with the majesty, significance, and subtlety of their first lines; one thinks especially of Virgil's *Arma virumque cano,* Lucretius'

Aeneadum genetrix, or Ovid's true opening line in the *Metamorphosis*—after four lines of typical persiflage—*Ante mare et terras et quod tegit omnia caelum.*)

That opening lines are important, even if they do not carry authorial self-consciousness, is clear from the opening of the *Iliad.* Every word of the first line of the *Iliad* conveys extremely important information to the hearer/reader:

Μῆνιν, ἄειδε, θεά, Πηληιάδεω 'Αχιλῆος

Sing, O goddess, the wrath of Achilles, son of Peleus.

The subject of the poem is Achilles' wrath, not his whole life nor his whole personality, much less the whole story of Troy (so the title *Iliad* is a serious mistake, a point made critically as early as Aristotle).[20] Indeed it is the tale of two sorts of wrath, a noisy wrath consisting of petulance and hurt pride over Agamemnon's insult, followed by a blacker, deeper, and all-consuming wrath, over the death of Patroclus, an event triggered by Achilles' indulgence of his earlier wrath again Agamemnon. The subject is then an emotion in the hero in one short period of time covered by a hugely ramified preexisting legend of the Trojan War cycle. In addition, the poet is saying that the wrath itself is a song, not just the subject of a song; that it preexists in a poetic tradition, having been sung before; and that a goddess has custody of it until and unless she chooses to impart it to a public through a singer or a bard. And, finally, the tragic element that lurks in all the corners of the *Iliad,* the fact that he, as son of Peleus, is also son of Thetis, who was fated to give birth to a son greater than his father, and has, by reason of his maternity, the choice of a long drab existence, or a short, glorious existence, and has opted for the latter. That Achilles' greatness, lesser than that of a god though greater than that of any other man, came to be because his mother was more or less forced to marry Peleus after Zeus discovered that the son of Thetis, by whatever sire, would be greater than his sire, is all implied in the first line of the *Iliad.* The first line of the

Iliad is an exquisitely more informative title for the poem than the raw abstraction *Iliad,* concocted hundreds of years after the fact, and based as it is on a dull pedant's notion of the subject of the poem.

All this, then, must make one take a harder lok at the first line of the *Odyssey* because it announces the theme of a man, not named ("Nobody"? Everybody?), with whom the poet is associated in nongrammatical proximity, who is the subject of many turnings (*polytropon*), and whose life is considered worthy of consideration quite apart from the emotions he has been subject to or the outcome of his projects and schemes. This, I suggest is not only a very different sort of program for an epic poem, it is very different sort of program for an epic poet.

The verb, finally, is not the Homeric one, "sing," *aeide,* but, as mentioned, a peculiar word, *ennepe,* meaning apparently *track down* or *search out.* This word has a moody quality to it, because the hero is of course lost as the poem opens and in fact does not appear until book 5, so that he is lost not just to his society, but to us the audience. At another level, if one were to read the *Odyssey* under the broadest possible literary criteria, then Odysseus remains to be found or sought out in a moral sense, too, for his own good, a task that involves perhaps more in the way of psychic threats and impositions on his life and character than the physical risks to which a hero in the *Iliad* is subject. In any case *ennepe* in no way means that the Muse is to sing the tale, through or alongside the poet, and I should say that it implies something altogether different in the way of relations between the poet and his Muse; rather like Demodocus or Hesiod, the poet needs, perhaps, information from the Muse, but not the substance of song, much less, remembering Odysseus' rhetorical question about the best ordering for a tale, her instructions in constructing that song. Given some such meaning as *search out* for the verb, then the pronoun translates *for me,* not *to me,* and that too constitutes a difference. The Muse is to assemble the raw materials for the song, while the poet is really to make it himself. These are significant departures from the practice seen in the first line of the *Iliad,* where the song, the *Menis,* is all. In the opening line of the *Odyssey* the subjects of the poem, in order of presentation, are first the man, second the personality of the poet (*moi*), third, the Muse, and fourth, instructions to her to find the man or track him down —so that the poet can begin to construct his own song about the hero? The pronoun stands between hero-subject and Muse-technique, as the arbiter, the producer-manager of the tale. As perhaps its author in almost a modern sense?

Finally, whether or not one wishes to see all that I do here in the selection and ordering of the words in the first line of the poem, at least a healthy fraction of what I have been maintaining would have been understood by anyone in antiquity hearing the poem as it now is, whether or not all this was planned at all or were the merest accident. For, as was noted, almost certainly, early poems were known by quoting their first line or first half-line. The poem later and rather lamely entitled *Iliad* was without doubt known in the first centuries of its existence as *Menin aeide thea*—"The Wrath, goddess, sing. . . ." Whatever may account for the condition the present first line of the *Odyssey* eventually took, it would have been known by that line and so referred to, and the presence of the pronoun *moi* in the second position between "Man" and "Muse" would inevitably have suggested to audiences familiar with the genre of epic a rising of self-assertion and vanity on the part of the poet. This, coupled with the subsequent attention and respect shown bards in the text, with the authority conferred upon them (snatched rudely away from priest and seer, and borrowed even from the hero), all would go to confirm the suspicion in the minds of the hearers that this poem had a status different from the *Iliad* or other known military epics, in the sense that its poet was making far more serious claims for recognition and reward for his social service, and indeed even for glory over which he even dares contend with his own hero.

Whether that same audience would go further and notice that the poet's poem draws a broader and more theoretical social lesson from its tale, namely the notion that social rank can be an evanescent thing and is no guarantee of virtue or wisdom—this I cannot attempt to guess with any degree of assurance. I think it obvious that the poet's great concern for his own status and that of his profession is related to a larger conviction that society in general rather routinely makes mistakes about the moral worth of men. The poem, at any rate, engages to a large degree in social wish-fulfillment, where useless aristocrats are destroyed and honest servants and unlucky men are rewarded, and that, I suspect, would have been equally hard to miss for an audience brought up on the Homer of the *Iliad*. There are so many gestures of sympathy and fellow-feeling to servants, peasants, the weak, and helpless in general; so many rebuffs to heroic social ritual (reenacted no doubt in rather shoddy form by the oligarchs of the poet's own day who claimed kinship with the heroes of the Trojan War); and, finally, so many celebrations of lower-class shrewdness in confrontation with upper-class hybris, which is shown to such disadvantage that it seems altogether probable that the poet's audiences did in fact associate the overall program of the poem, the dismantling of heroic notions of human worth, with the personal subplot the poet employs to magnify and exalt his profession and call attention to his status and artistic worthiness. The *Odyssey* is the poem of wit and plan as against automatic courage and nobility in the traditional forms, where courage and rudeness and bravado are all synonymous, the bane of a peasant's existence. We, living too long since the ages of peasant and noble, have perhaps collectively forgotten that wit is traditionally the weapon of the peasant against the noble, a psychic defense against the nobles' snobbery as well as a practical defense against their impositions. One may well ask if the wit and scheming evident in the *Odyssey* are not, coequally, weapons forged to use against both the effortless nobility as well as the snobbery, of the *Iliad*.

Notes

1. *See* D. L. Page, *The Homeric Odyssey* (Oxford: Oxford University Press 1955), pp. 84–87, though he notes that at the end of book 20 Theoclymenus makes an accurate enough prophecy of the Suitors' demise (easy enough to do), which is "some compensation for his dismal past"; on the consultation with Teirisias see pp. 27–32.

2. *Iliad* 9.186 ff.

3. *See* Brooks Otis, *Virgil: A Study in Civilized Poetry* (Oxford: Oxford University Press 1963), pp. 239 ff.: The narration of the fall of Troy given by Aeneas in books 2 and 3 is a "subjective" account, indicating the degree to which Aeneas both understands and accepts his past—this psychological element has radically changed the character of first-person narrative, which is no longer an exercise in talent, as in the *Odyssey*, but a device for the hero's self-revelation. It may be doubted whether Virgil was equipped to understand the ambiguous situation of Odysseus posing as a poet. Like everyone else in his day, Virgil must naturally have assumed that the *Odyssey* was a written work, and thus he proceeded to make the narration of Aeneas a self-revealing document because that is what he assumed *Odyssey* books 9–11 were. It would be interesting—if far beyond the scope of this book—to compare the two narrations to see, if possible, how Virgil read Homer, in explicit detail.

4. The implication of Helen's words to Paris in *Iliad* 6.357–58, that they two will be *aoidimoi* (*singable*) in future times, is that great stories of important people will irresistibly force themselves into the body of song that records the epic world and its doings. There is no indication that any particular bard, or any significant talent, are required for this to happen.

5. *See* D. J. N. Lee, *Similes of the Iliad and the Odyssey Compared* (Melbourne: Melbourne University Press 1964), pp. 2–7, 28–29. *See also* pp. 10–11: Lee compares the similes of the *Odyssey* to "green lights" that pass traffic through to literary meaning (that is, they are really symbols), while he compares most of the similes of the *Iliad* to "red lights" that halt traffic, call attention to themselves for their arbitrariness, and do not advance the narrative.

6. *Tusculan Disputations* 1.15, 1.34.

7. The Serbian bard Demail Zogic told Milman Parry that the singer should sing his tale "as he heard it, and as things happen"; quoted from G. S. Kirk, *Language and Background of Homer* (Cambridge and New York: Cambridge University Press 1964), p. 83. *See also* Aristotle, *Poetics* 1459 b, and E. Delebecque, *Télémaque et la structure de l'Odyssee* (Paris: Editions Ophrys 1958), pp. 125 ff.

8. *See* A. B. Lord, *The Singer of Tales* (New York: Harvard University Press 1968), pp. 27 ff., 69 ff., 104–6; 127–28, 154–56.

9. *Hymn to Delian Apollo*, line 172.

10. If the oral tradition was unlikely to have supplied the poet of the *Odyssey* with ready-made passages praising poets and poetry, it was still less likely to have supplied him or any poet with the materials of a

"song within a song" like the Song of the Sirens, that is, *direct quotations* of other songs, here delivered by immortals. In a way, the Song of the Sirens is even more daring, in metaphysical status if not in scope, than the song of Demodocus about Ares and Aphrodite, which was reported only in *indirect* quotation.

11. *See* Albin Lesky, *A History of Greek Literature,* trans. J. Willis and C. de Heer (New York: Thomas Y. Crowell Co., 1966), p. 65; and A. B. Lord, p. 150.

12. *See* W. J. Woodhouse, *The Composition of Homer's Odyssey* (Oxford: Clarendon Press 1930), pp. 11–15; E. R. Dodds, "Homer" in *Fifty Years of Classical Scholarship,* ed. M. Platnauer (Oxford: : Oxford University Press 1954), p. 8.

13. *See* Lord, pp. 124–25.

14. The lines in praise of Demodocus in book 8 make the following points: he is famous (8.367); he, and all good poets, deserve honors among all men, because the Muse has taught them song and has loved (or "kissed"—*philēse*) them (8.477–81); Odysseus singles him out for superlative praise, among all men, because he has been taught, either by Apollo and the Muses or by experience itself, and can sing the songs of Troy properly and truly (8.487–491); if he can tell the story of the Wooden Horse, Odysseus stands ready to tell the world that a wise god had made the song (8.496–498). The praise of the poet's Muse in the beginning of the speech is conventional; the mounting praise of the poet in and for himself, is far from it. In book 1.351–2 Telemachus implies that poets are capable of originality, not just the handing on of their tradition; at 22.347–8, Phemius claims to be self-taught.

15. This and the following translation of Hesiod's *Theogony* are from H. D. Evelyn-White, *Hesiod, the Homeric Hymns and Homerica,* The Loeb Classical Library (London and Cambridge, Mass.: Harvard University Press 1954).

16. *See* M. L. West, ed., *Hesiod, Theogony* (Oxford: Oxford University Press 1966), pp. 40, 47 ff. (Introduction.) In the commentary, at line 22, West writes: "The poet names himself in the third person, not to set his signature upon the poem (this can not have been necessary at a time when there was no circulation of written books), but rather out of simple pride. . . ." To me, this is a distinction without a difference. On p.48 West argues that Hesiod wrote his poem down just to have it near him, for ready reference if called upon to sing it, yet eight pages earlier he acknowledges that the poem did circulate, and rather speedily at that. To me, West has not reached a very settled picture of why he thinks Hesiod wrote, or for whom. It seems to me that a poem based on the thesis that the Muses can tell either the truth or lies ((lines 27–28), is a polemical poem (whatever the target), intended for as wide a circulation as the writer thereof can manage or imagine for it, not just for chance hearers with whom the poet may come into physical contact. Since, as West himself says, the *Theogony* spread rapidly "across the seas," surely it was designed to do just that, in which case Hesiod's use of his name

is a signature designed to keep his poem from being appropriated by others and its message from being thus contaminated.

17. *See* Herodotus 2, 116 for the word *Iliad;* 4, 29 for the word *Odyssey.*

18. *See* West, p. 150.

19. A. W. Gomme, *Historical Commentary on Thucydides* vol. 4 (Oxford: Oxford University Press 1959), 1 : 89.

20. *Poetics* 1451a. *See also* Lord (note 8 above) pp. 99–100, p. 286, n. 2, on the practice of naming poems by first lines among Serbian bards.

Appendix

Drugs in the Odyssey

THE *ODYSSEY* PROVIDES A FASCINATING LOOK AT CONSCIOUSNESS-altering drugs, whether known or simply imagined, that is virtually unique in ancient literature. Later tellings of ancient myth seem to have screened out nearly all such materials, while retaining accounts of drugs that are de facto poisons, like the blood of Nessus or Medea's incendiary venoms.

It is peculiar that little or no work has been done on the drug "scene" in this poem—perhaps it has required the emergence of a half-open drug scene in the present era to call live attention to the drugs in the *Odyssey*. (The difference here is not one of burgeoning drug use, but of new frankness in talking about it. All ages have used drugs, evidently, but most of the time drugs were called by other names and thus no public consensus to admit the prevalence of drugs as a social fact existed. John Fowles's superb novel *The French Lieutenant's Woman* makes this very point for the Victorian era; drug use, he shows, was probably more widespread, both in the total number of users as well as across all social classes, than today, but this was disguised by the fact that they were called *patent medicines* in many cases, such as laudanum and chloral hydrate.) At any rate, it seems that this topic deserves some little attention since it has a real if modest effect on the plot of the *Odyssey*.

To be sure, there is no absolute need to connect any of the drugs in the *Odyssey* with any real drugs at all. All could be figments of one or several poet's imaginations, but that does not matter greatly because the one thing no number of Homers could have imagined was the sheer existence of drugs in the first place. He or they had to know the class of drugs even to invent new and imaginary ones. And thus, whether observed or imagined, these drugs come to the same thing in terms of narrative aims. The point of attempting to approximate these drugs to modern known drugs is to explicate the variety of clinical effects the poet describes in some detail. The descriptions are not all the same, and do not all mean the same thing. That fact in itself is a good reason for asking how close they come to resembling real known drugs in the present era.

I first began thinking about the subject of drugs in the *Odyssey** while digesting W. S. Anderson's essay, "Calypso and Elysium," referred to in chapter 1. I was especially struck then by his remarks on Helen's drug *nēpenthē* and how her use of it signals a serious collapse in the relationship between her and Menelaus:

> In Sparta husband and wife must cast a veil over the past, try to forget the circumstances which brought first Helen, then Menelaus to Troy, merely recall events as adventures which have no bearing upon the present. Oblivion does not come easily, for human feelings go deep and the scars of the past do not disappear. Therefore to create the ideal conditions for reception of her evocation of the past, Helen must use a drug. Even that drug cannot put to sleep the emotions of Menelaus nor, I suspect, those of Helen. (p. 76)

I do not happen to think that this relationship is in any way so innocent as Anderson sees it: Helen and Menelaus have no intention of recalling events in the past simply as adventures, and in fact they use memory as a weapon. But, and here I am more at one with Anderson, so that resentment will not reach fatal conclusions, and yet the pathological game of innuendo go

* Using C. R. B. Joyce, ed. *Psychopharmacology: Dimensions and Perspectives* (London: J. B. Lippincot, 1968), references are given in parentheses to editor's name and page number.

on indefinitely, *nēpenthē* is administered to blunt temptations to actual violence or to completely frank accusations. What concerns me here is Anderson's comprehension that the drug had nothing to do with Telemachus or his problems, nor with Menelaus' self-proclaimed love for the lost Odysseus (which I, for one, do not think the poet expects one to believe); the drug is a form of self-indulgence and self-protection used by Helen primarily to protect herself : she needs it to calm her own anger and anguish; but Menelaus also needs it, so that his anger will not go so far as to threaten her safety. And even Telemachus, conceivably, might end up blaming her as the ultimate cause of his father's absence.

From these considerations I was led to remember—really to see in a new pattern—the other cases of drug use that punctuate the text of the *Odyssey*. Here follows a brief resume of the drug passages in the text of the poem. In book 4 Helen, as noted, uses a drug, usually called *nēpenthē,* to prevent sadness overcoming the participants at a dinner party for Telemachus, and then leading to anger. They are discussing the old days, but Helen and Menelaus use reminiscence to rake one another's souls with mutual recriminations, and so an anodyne seems helpful to keep a social occasion respectable. From the evidence given in the text I should say that *nēpenthē* to some extent resembles cocaine in its actions, but even more closely, Rauwolfia. In book 9, early in the Adventures, Odysseus meets the Lotus-eaters, a good-natured people who freely offer Lotus, their special food, to all comers. Lotus induces forgetfulness of all political and social allegiences in strangers, like Odysseus' crew, even though in some way the Lotus society seems to cohere with itself. It is a utopian drug, making one insensitive to the threat-plus-reward system of inducing social conformity, though, again, Lotus society exhibits a different type of conformity. Clearly, it negates what we thing of as history, as well as careers. From clinical evidence, from the busy journalism of self-proclaimed users, from reports of events like Woodstock in the press, it would seem clear that Lotus, if real, is a cannabis-type drug, a near-relative of marijuana or hashish. In book 10 Circe uses some kind of drug upon her guests that first robs them of their purpose to return home and then turns them, with the help of magic incantations, into animals. Some of Odysseus' men are so victimized, but Odysseus himself, forewarned and forearmed by Hermes with a different drug, *moly*, is able to overcome Circe's chemical expertise. Upon their first confrontation, Odysseus is unaffected by Circe's drug and, to a degree, forces her to do his bidding. Circe's drug, at least in part, seems to resemble an hallucinogen like LSD. It is hard to say what Hermes' *moly* is. Except for chlorpromazine, a modern synthetic tranquilizing agent, there does not seem to be any antidote. to hallucinogens known to the modern pharmacopia, and *moly* is clearly an antidote. It is a plant "of black root and white flower" (book 10.304), words that probably in themselves do not mean a great deal, but it is also very had to pluck from the ground (10.305–6), and only a god, Hermes, can do it easily. This suggests that possibly folk etymology is at work here. *Moly* is described as a tranquilizing agent, and has the connotations of heaviness and stability. The same lexical root, at least by the standards of Greek popular etymology, would have been seen by the Greeks themselves in their words *molybdos* (the metal lead), *molis* (adverb, "with difficulty"), *molos* (a long and heavy struggle; battle is the "*molos* of Ares" in *Iliad* 2.401), and *mule* (millstone : compare Latin *mola* or *molis,* a heavy weight or a struggle). The idea of *moly* as a controlling agent, an antidote, is the primary sense recognized in the *Etymologicum Magnum* :

moly . . . from the verb *moluein,* (that is "to soften" or "to control")—controlling destructive feelings.

Moluein has a number of medical usages attested in Liddell and Scott's Greek Lexicon, generally having to do with controlling or checking bodily or psychic excesses. The plant *moly* combines the aspect of "control," better recognized in later antiquity, with that of "weightiness," which is probably the principle connotation in Homer's mind. Here the poet probably has no specific drug in mind, but it simply inventing one. He is guessing that the antidote to Circe's drug, whatever it is, should be heavy, like an anchor, weighing a man's mind down and tying it to earth and the consciousness of inescapable realities. Thus *moly* may not define itself very clearly, but by contrast it helps define the nature of Circe's drug. If *moly* is heavy and down-to-earth, Circe's potion must be the agent of an elative and ecstatic experience (ecstatic not in the sense of joyous, but in the original Greek sense of "standing outside," an extra-personal "trip" outside the self—her victims stand outside human nature, though they retain human consciousness). Therefore a hallucinogen, something like LSD or mescaline is probably what Circe was using.

There are two other possible cases of the employment of drugs in the *Odyssey,* The first is the wine used by Odysseus to subdue the Cyclops. The second is involved with the whole problem of book 11, the trip to the Underworld—in book 11 one might fairly ask whether real time passes, whether there is a real voyage, or is at all a different kind of hallucinatory "trip?"

Nēpenthē. In book 4, Helen and Menelaus, in response to the quest of their guests Telemachus and Eurylochus, begin to recall the past—and to rake up old sore points in doing so. Helen, who is not pictured as generally decisive, decides that this could cause a great deal of trouble unless everyone present is induced, chemically, to forget not so much past events themselves, as the pain, anger, or irritation that such recollections would normally bring. She determines to blunt the edge of remembered pain, by drugging the entire company :

> And so, then, Helen, daughter of Zeus, took thought of another course. Straightway she threw a drug into the wine they were drinking, a substance that negates pain and anger, that makes one forget all troubles. Whoever should consume it mixed in his cup, would never shed a tear—he a mere mortal, creature of a day—no, not even if his mother or father should die, or his brother or son be slaughtered before his very eyes.
>
> (4.219–26)

"A substance that negates pain and anger," *pharmakon* . . . *nēpenthes t' acholon*—for convenience generally called *nēpenthē*, "no pain," though *acholos* or *acholia*, "no anger," would do as well. From the context it is clear that *nēpenthē* reduces combativeness and self-assertion almost completely, while still permitting the person under its influence to continue to function socially, to converse, remember (but not the anger of remembrance; "oblivion," *pace* Anderson, is not quite what Helen is after), and pass the time of day. It is not like alcohol or barbiturates : no one goes to sleep or retreats into depression. Nor, as with marijuana, is everyone giddy, distracted, or tempted to "drop out" of his social role. It can hardly be opium, as Hayman argued in his *Odyssey* edition of 1866–82, for it has nothing to do with dreams or illusions. It is very much a businessman's drug. It allows one to carry on in almost any social context without experiencing emotional pain or anger (apparently physical sensations are not altered at all). It most clearly resembles the action of either cocaine, or Rauwolfia, or the synthetic tranquilizer chlorpromazine (Joyce, pp. 123–25). Since we must be dealing here with a natural substance, the latter can be excluded from consideration, and cocaine seems to have no other known source that the coca leaf of South America, so it too can probably be excluded. Rauwulfia, however, stems from India, and has been used there, apparently forever, by practitioners of folk medicine to treat otherwise uncontrollable anger and potential aggressiveness, both in cases of single criminals and in family feuds! (Joyce, ibid.). It first came to the professional-medical attention of Europe in the seventeenth century, but its frequent rediscoveries since then by the West (Joyce, ibid.) suggests that this has been a periodic phenomenon, and that it has made its way to Europe more than once or twice in history, and no doubt did so in antiquity as well. It certainly seems to have the effects described, with some sarcasm, by the poet here.

Lotus. Homer's description of the Lotus-eaters is striking, but one should not forget that they have gained a long-standing notoriety out of all proportion to the amount of attention the poem actually gives them. In exchange for exactly twenty lines of epic text the Lotus-eaters have acquired a unique immortality as an all-purpose political and moral cliche. They have become a rhetorical convenience to be dragged forward in and out of season by all sorts of partisans whenever public debate moves from patriotic and warlike themes to the question of how men should live to be happy.

For specifics, there are these facts. The Lotus-eaters show neither hostility nor any great interest toward their visitors —which is unique enough among all the hosts Odysseus and his crew have to face (book 9.92–93). They give of the *lōtos* freely to all comers (9.93–94). This immediately makes the sailors want to stay behind, because it induces forgetfulness of home, of duty toward authority, and of any sense of earned social role (9.95–97). Yet the same men offer no resistance when Odysseus drives them back to the ship and their obligatory roles (9.98–99) —they only weep. The prime effect of *lōtos*—to Odysseus the great captain—is forgetting about the homecoming (9.102), but other effects are worthy of attention.

The Lotus-eaters are placid and passive. Assuming that they are living where they have always lived, the prime effect, for them, is not forgetting some other homeland but their strange peace and gentleness. They are an uncontentious and concessive people, yet they are not anarchists—they have a society of sorts, which seems to work well enough to suit them. (And, to his credit, Odysseus does not victimize them.) The drug then appears to be a mild euphoriant like marijuana or hashish, and the general picture one gets of the life conditions of the *lōtos* eaters may indeed resemble the admittedly self-serving arguments of promarijuana spokesmen in our day, picturing a delightful utopian society that somehow meets practical needs without compulsion or aggression. To Odysseus, as mentioned, the prime effects are a subversion of good order and political discipline. In this respect—a clash of two very different views of social structure, and of fundamental styles of consciousness—the similarity of *lōtos* and the hemp derivatives seems very close indeed (Joyce, pp. 194–95). It is clear enough that this was Homer's intention in using the episode : he is primarily interested in contrasting opposed views of history and society.

In this case one must also remember that the Homeric portrait of Lotus society as mild and nonaggressive, simply because of its remarkable propaganda value down through the ages, has worked its inevitable effects even on today's publicists for the cult of marijuana. Given the need to say something in defense of the drug—whatever its value for the individual—one can surmise that its proponents have been tempted to make more spacious claims, namely that marijuana is a social panacea, simply because a social justification seems so much more persuasive than a merely personal and private defense. Yet in the very act of doing just this they demonstrate how much they are under the influence of the tradition of Lotus rhetoric. Only they have turned that tradition back upon itself, and have used it to deny the virtue of work and ambition, as much as to undermine the argument that euphoria and inactivity are irresponsible and dangerous—which has been the traditional position of those who have successfully used anti-Lotus rhetoric to maintain the opposite and more familiar thesis, that anything which weakens the claims of duty and compulsion is a dangerous threat to society. Both rhetorical intentions are obviously quite elusive of proof, which is probably what makes them so attractive and seductive. It would appear that on the social performance of euphoriant drugs the clinician, the journalist, and the public philosopher are equally at a loss.

Circe's drug. Circe in book 10 uses drugs to change men into animals. The story represents the confluence of a better-recognized magical tradition, with a drug tradition that is not so well recognized. Witches are best known in all folklore for changing people—including themselves—into animals. But Circe does not depend solely on spells, incantations, or magical devices like wands to change men; she uses a potion. And Odysseus uses a different magic, also a drug apparently, to counteract her drug. The scene is a mixture of cultural themes. It is therefore at least plausible to suggest that what we have here is the conflation of magic and an imperfectly understood hallicinogen. Maybe Odysseus' men only imagine that they are turned into beasts—despite the extreme detail of ocular evidence Odysseus gives about their appearance, to him. He, after all, may not be entirely free of secondary or unnoticed narcotic effects of Circe's drug, though through his antidote he seems to escape the primary effects of being changed into an animal himself. For there is a class of hallucinogens known as *anticholinergics* that can induce just these symptoms: forgetfulness of one's identity, auditory effects (not known in the cannabis, or mescaline—LSD groups), and visions of animals! (Joyce, pp. 200–203). Most of the known anticholinergics are synthetic, but one group, the piperidyl benzilates (Joyce, p. 199) are found in natural substances. Perhaps Odysseus' men are affected by a cannabis-type hallucinogen stronger than simple marijuana ("changes in body-image are frequent"—Joyce, p. 194), while Odysseus himself is affected by an anticholinergic.

The Cyclops' wine. There are two other passages that may be further examples of drug use, though these cases are problematic and the evidence is circumstantial only. Moreover these two cases form a separate group, because, if indeed the use of drugs is at issue in these places, their use is as a device for controlling the behavior of another who does *not* know he has been drugged; that is, he never quite understands what has been done to him. (Circe's victims, beforehand, are unaware of her drug, but after the act, they comprehend what she has done, and how she has done it; this is in fact a part of her triumph.)

The first of these cases has to do with the wine that Odysseus offers the Cyclops, Polyphemus (book 9.347 ff.). This wine must be terribly strong, since two drinks suffice to stupefy the monster. Yet the Cyclopes knew wine (book 9.110), and it is hard to understand how this wine, no matter how strong relative to ordinary men, could have subdued the monster so quickly (after the first drink Polyphemus himself says: we Cyclopes know wine well enough . . . but this is something different, a compound of ambrosia and nectar—9.357–59). A passage in the introductory remarks Odysseus gives the Phaeacians before getting to the Cyclops-story proper, which explains this peculiar wine, merits attention. Odysseus says he landed on the isle of the Cyclopes, picked twelve good men as companions, and set out to explore the place. He then adds,

> . . . But I had a goatskin full of dark wine, which Maron son of Euanthes had given me . . .
> . . . It was a divine potion nor did any of his maids or servants know of it, but only himself, his wife and one stewardess. And when they drank this red and honeyed drink they would mix it with water at a twenty-to-one ration. . . . (9.196–210)

This passage is recognized as late and intrusive, a device concocted by a rather pedantic later poet, to account for the instant intoxication of the Cyclops later in the book. The word *But,* used to introduce the passage, is an adversative to nothing, while the name *Maron son of Euanthes* is in the nature of an etymological insinuation. Not knowing quite what to make of the Cyclops' sudden befuddlement when he drinks the "wine," whoever composed this resorts to experimental aetiology. It is, first, the wine of a man called *Maron.* One may compare the verb *maraino,* stem *maran-, to weaken.* Maron is the son of Euanthes, meaning *good flower* (there is some thought of botanical drugs here, clearly). The interpellator is struggling with a difficulty : he understands that the condition of the Cyclops is not quite natural, but he can not quite imagine just what is wrong with him, or the drink. In addition, the stated ratio of 20 to 1, water to wine, is both an exact figure and a puzzling one. That the Greeks drank their wine mixed with water is well known. Ratios from 2 : 1 to 5 : 1 were also well known (see Hesiod, *Works and Days,* 556). But a ratio of 20 : 1 looks either like a deliberate invasion of fantasy—or an invitation to suspect the presence of drugs. The wine of Ismarus, moreover, even if it should be drunk at a ratio of 20 : 1 with water by mere men, should hardly affect the Cyclops as it does given his size, unless it is actually a drugged wine, not just wine pure and simple. The Cyclops, after all, must be between 10 and 20 times normal human size, so the special potency of the wine should be pretty much cancelled out. Toxicity is in inverse ratio to body weight for all known toxins, and one can imagine that even the ancient Greeks would have had some empirical glimmering of this fact. Although, soon after Homer, a cultural conspiracy of silence appears to have closed down any free expression of opinion and observation about narcotic drugs it is clear that the Greeks continued to think and speculate very freely on the subject of poisons and stimulants and knew, with fair precision, how to assess and predict clinical effects. There is, in the latter case, not just the evidence of tragedy (Sophocles' *Trachiniae,* and Euripides' *Medea*) but also that of Plato's *Phaedo* (117b–e); according to which, the lethal draught of hemlock that Socrates had to drink was so precisely measured —how, one wonders, unless the magistrates had calculated his weight—that he could not spill out even a drop or two as a religious offering or the drug will not work properly. Thus the possibility exists that one should view this wine as a concoction treated with a soporific drug, a natural barbiturate, perhaps, or opium, and not just as wine, nor even "brandy," as Fitzgerald, sensing the difficulty, as translated it.

Odysseus' trip. At the end of book 10, Circe tells Odysseus that he must go to the Underworld to learn from the ghost of Teirisias how he is to proceed home. Page has shown that this is a fruitless errand, at least for the stated purpose, because (1) Teirisias gives Odysseus no such information, and (2) when he returns to Circe's island from the Underworld, Odysseus finds that Circe had all along had the information that Teirisias alone was supposedly able to give. The beginning of book 12 thus makes it appear that to its author, book 11 had never existed.

Is this a case of faulty editing plus egregious interpolation, or is the poet trying to tell us that Odysseus has never really gone anywhere, that he has really had a dream, or has been hypnotized, or has only been on a chemical "trip?" This may sound, at first, like a bizarre and idiosyncratic interpretation, but let us consider a few circumstances surrounding the trip itself. The prelude to the visit to the Underworld comes at the end of book 10. Odysseus' crewmen after a year of wining and dining with Circe, confront their leader with a demand that he remember his own avowed purpose and set about getting them home (10.472–74). At this point it is he, not they, who is so charmed by something about Circe's hospitality that he has almost forgotten his purpose. The crew, returned from animal status, are no longer affected, apparently, by any form of drug or enchantment. The same may not be true of Odysseus. Odysseus agrees that he should do something, and that night in Circe's bed he asks her to remember her promise to set them free (10.480–86). She is agreeable: he and his men do not have to stay in her halls any longer (10.489), but to return home they must first proceed to Hades to learn their way from the all-wise Teirisias (10.490–95). Hearing this Odysseus is crushed with despair:

> . . . my heart was torn within me. And I wept as I clutched the bed, and my soul no longer wished to live or see the light of day. But when finally I had had my fill of wailing and tossing, I said to Circe, 'Who will lead us on the way, since no one before has reached Hades by ship.'
>
> (10.496–501)

Now this development in the story is curious. First, Odysseus had to be reminded by his men about returning home, and one wonders if he were all that willing to go. But he agrees. Then Circe sets a frightening condition: he must first go to Hades. Hell of course is a fearful place, one supposes, but Circe does not seem to imply that its generally fearful aspects will pose any threat to Odysseus when, he goes there for this specific purpose. So far as her words tell it, he will be going there for information, and nothing more. Why then, though the proposal is odd enough, does it take Odysseus so completely by storm that he apparently has an attack or fit of some kind that keeps him rolling and groaning most of the night? His behavior here to some extent resembles the withdrawal symptoms of those who have become addicted to certain euphoriant drugs. Has Circe kept her guests for a year by feeding them—or at least Odysseus—some form of unguessed narcotic? The possibility exists. Although Odysseus thinks he has put a stop to her use of the drug that turns men into beasts, she may well have been using something else from her stock of dangerous chemicals that worked just as well to subdue them and keep them around her. Remember, Odysseus appears to have forgotten his home in all that time, and forgetfulness was also a phenomenon produced by eating *lōtos*. Moreover, Odysseus seems addicted to something about Circe's table. He enjoys just a bit too much telling of their daily feasts,

> and there, every day for a full year we reclined and con-
> sumed indescribable food and the sweetest wine.
> (10.467–68)

The same enthusiasm is then repeated a few lines further on. After the last great meal, where Odysseus claims,

> . . . we sat and consumed indescribable food and the sweet-
> est wine . . .
> (10.477)

he finally asks Circe for permission to depart. Could it be that Circe has been drugging her guests all along?

The trip to the Underworld itself shows some signs of having been a drug experience. For instance, there is Circe's—and the poem's—behavior at the completion of the adventure, as if no real trip had taken place at all. Then, there is the question of elapsed time, which is very puzzling indeed. According to Odysseus, the journey from Aeaea to the gates of Hades took at least twenty-four hours, and, realistically, probably a great deal longer. The trip began promptly at dawn of the morning after Odysseus had his nightlong fit (10.11–12), and as night falls he and his men are still sailing, and sail on until they reach Oceanus, the river girdling the world, "where the tribe and state of the Cimmerians is." This is the Black Sea area and beyond, going east. The trip started, so far as one can tell, in the Adriatic, where most people place Aeaea. (It is simply not true, as Page would have it, that Aeaea is "at the eastern limits of the world" [*The Homeric Odyssey*, p. 21]; Aeaea for the ancients was more or less where Virgil placed it, in or near the Adriatic—compare *Aeneid* 7. 10–24. If Aeaea were in the east, then the time-length of this voyage would be too long, not too short.) The collapsing of apparent distances is a common phenomenon produced by the hallucinogens (Joyce, p. 194). Odysseus, however, is even more hazy about time than space. Apparently Odysseus and his men sail on for most of the night—or longer. There, at the fringes of the world, there is continual gloom and no sun shines (11.15–19), so who can tell how many "days" they kept on sailing. But, to him, it was at least one full day and the better half of the night, even allowing for the most fanciful geography. Yet, on their return, Odysseus is careful to note, they reached Aeaea on *the morning following* their departure (12.5–7). Thus, even if one is very lenient with the text, a trip that takes at the very least twenty-four hours going out, then takes no more time at all for the round trip. This is a most elastic and obliging universe! The unreality of this time sequence has an outward and objective excuse. Elpenor, one of Odysseus' crew, who was not very bright anyway, got drunk at the last banquet and went to sleep on the roof of Circe's palace (10.552 ff.). He awoke the next morning, and not quite knowing where he was, stepped off the roof, fell to the ground and died of a broken neck. His companions meanwhile had left for the Underworld without him (and apparently without wondering where he was). The first ghost Odysseus meets in the Underworld is this same Elpenor (11.51 ff.), who begs his captain to give him a decent funeral (perhaps in parody of Patroclus' demand for a timely funeral in the *Iliad*). Then, when Odysseus returns to Aeaea his first thoughts and words are for this pious duty toward the dead (12.9ff.). Now why Elpenor, of all unlikely people, has earned this high degree of recognition in the poem is very difficult to say on the face of things. He is one of only a very few members of Odysseus's crew who even earns a name from the poet, and he has nothing whatever, besides this episode, to distinguish him, a fact that gave Girandoux the excuse to write his extremely funny novella *Elpénor*. But given his very short literary existence it is clear in one sense, why the trip to the Underworld is completed in Alice-in-Wonderland time. It would not do for the expedition to return on a more realistic schedule and find that they have to do honor to a corpse that had been moldering anywhere from four days to six weeks! There is very little realism in this whole adventure, but one may say that the corpse of Elpénor provides the one realistic control by which to judge all the other apparent facts in this adventure. The corpse of Elpénor is still fresh, fresh enough not to cause comment, and it makes one think, though very tentatively, that maybe there was no trip to the Underworld at all, except in the drugged mind of Odysseus, which need not, in any way, reduce the validity of his experiences on that trip.

Now what is one to make—what does Homer make—of all this? First of all, that drugs are dangerous, obviously. But, second, that they are not always dangerous to the same people for the same reasons. Helen's *nēpenthē,* as Anderson shows, is a sad requisite as well as a symbol of the wretched immortality she and Menelaus face together, and is effectively set against a countersymbol, Odysseus' refusal to live forever with Calypso, even to enjoy an oblivious immortality of his own. Yet, Helen's drug is apparently necessary for her and Menelaus. Without it their catty acrimony would no doubt reach a really homicidal level. They have too much memory for their own good, and *nēpenthē* blocks the natural results of having memories, the desire to relive the feelings that memory contains. *Nēpenthē* unhooks memory from its usual consequences. *Lōtos,* on the other hand, destroys memory altogether or at least all memory of pre-*lōtos* existence. Here is the more fundamental attitude of the poet based not on an abstract theory about drugs themselves but on his concern for memory : memory of home, of dear ones, of happy times and great deeds is a fundamental good for the poet, and indeed it is these that hold together the social order—if they do—and make it worthy. (And, at another level, memory is crucial for art, obviously.) Thus, since drugs on the whole threaten or distort memory, they are bad; they rob a man of that which makes him civilized, and in some cases simply keeps him safe. Even wine can be dangerous. Elpenor drank too much and forgot where he was; and even if the Cyclops was stupefied by nothing stronger than wine without additive drugs, it still made him vulnerable. The Suitors of Penelope, too, drunk more or less permanently on hybris, but also frequently on wine, are forgetful of their general danger and even sometimes of very specific warnings and omens. And Circe's drugs made even Odysseus forgetful of home, to the point that his crew had to remind him of it. Yet on the other hand the poet concedes that memory is probably not always a good thing for everyone everywhere. On balance Helen and Menelaus are probably better off with their drugs. And the poet has no word of explicit condemnation for the *lōtos*-eaters —nor even for Odysseus' men who succumb to their drug (the point is not major, but it is worth observing that if some of Odysseus' crewmen had been permitted to stay and become citizens of Lotus land, later on they might not have been eaten by the Cyclops, nor would they have eaten the cattle of Helios and perished for their crime in a storm at sea). Still, by and large the poet is inimical to drugs that induce oblivion : they take away from man that which the poet considers his chief mark of excellence, his ability to learn and retain experience, and then to build from retained experience a better existence, a better character, or a better culture.

If book 11 is a hallucinogenic "trip" and not a real one,

then the poet's point of view here is slightly different. The poet is generally in favor of new, and even trying, experience, not so much because he thinks that adventure is in itself very important except that it is yet another opportunity to know and learn still more about the objective world, and knowledge is never bad. Odysseus' real *aristeia* in the poem is not to win battles but to learn "the minds of many men," even of dead men. The trip to the underworld, real or not, was a singularly important educational experience for the hero—perhaps the most profound of all. The traditional view of the first four books of the poem, the *Telemachia,* takes it to be a book of education, a *Bildungsroman.* What the critical tradition has largely neglected is the fact that the whole poem is a *Bildungsroman* for the older man, the father of Telemachus. This being the case, one could imagine the poet deciding that drugs, too, are a part of experience, and maybe one could learn even from them. And, that being granted, given the poem's frequent points of contact with a drug culture of some kind, it is not altogether implausible that in book 11 the poet conducts his hero on a hallucinogenic trip to the Underworld precisely when and where it will do him the most good. But only then, and for very special reasons, does it earn something like his grudging acceptance.

Bibliography

Amory, Anne. "The Reunion of Odysseus and Penelope." In *Essays on the Odyssey,* edited by C. H. Taylor. Bloomington, Ind.: Indiana University Press, 1963.

Anderson, W. S. "Calypso and Elysium." In *Essays on the Odyssey,* edited by C. H. Taylor. Bloomington, Ind.: Indiana University Press, 1963.

Auerbach, Erich. *Mimesis.* Translated by Willard Trask. Princeton, N.J.: Princeton University Press, 1953.

Beye, C. R. *The Iliad, The Odyssey, and the Epic Tradition.* New York: Doubleday, 1966.

Carpenter, Rhys. *Folk Tale, Fiction, and Saga in the Homeric Epics.* Berkeley and Los Angeles: University of California Press, 1946.

Delébecque, E. *Telémaque et la structure de l'Odyssee.* Paris: Editions Ophrys, 1958.

Dodds, E. R. "Homer." In *Fifty Years of Classical Scholarship,* edited by M. Platnauer. Oxford: Basil Blackwell, 1954.

Donaldson, E. T., trans. *Beowulf.* New York: W. W. Norton Co., 1966.

Evelyn-White, H. D., ed. & trans. *Hesiod, the Homeric Hymns and Homerica.* The Loeb Classical Library. London and Cambridge, Mass.: Wm. Heinemann and Harvard University Press, 1954.

Fitzgerald, Robert, trans. *Odyssey.* New York: Doubleday & Co., 1961.

Frazer, J. E., ed & trans. *Apollodorus*. The Loeb Classical Library. London: Wm. Heinemann, 1931.

Gomme, A. W. *Historical Commentary on Thucydides*. Vol. 1. Oxford: Oxford University Press, 1959.

———, "Homer." In *More Essays in Greek History and Literature*. Oxford: Basil Blackwell, 1962.

Hackman, Oskar. *Die Polyphemsage in der Volküberlieferung*. Helsingfors: Frenckellska tryckeriaktiebolaget, 1904.

Harsh, P. W. "Penelope and Odysseus in the *Odyssey*." *American Journal of Philology* 71 (1950): 1–21.

Kirk, G. S. *Language and Background of Homer*. Cambridge and New York: Cambridge University Press, 1964.

Lee, D. J. N. *Similes of the Iliad and the Odyssey Compared*. Melbourne: Melbourne University Press, 1964.

Lesky, Albin. *History of Greek Literature*. Translated by J. Willis and C. deHeer. New York: Thomas Y. Crowell Co., 1966.

Levy, H. L. "The Odyssean Suitors and the Host-Guest Relationship." *Transactions of the American Philological Association* 94 (1963): 145–53.

Lord, A. B. *The Singer of Tales*. Cambridge, Mass.: Harvard University Press, 1960.

Otis, Brooks. *Virgil: A Study in Civilized Poetry*. Oxford: Oxford University Press, 1963.

Page, Denys. *The Homeric Odyssey*. Oxford: Oxford University Press, 1955.

———. *History and the Homeric Iliad*. Berkeley and Los Angeles: University of California Press, 1963.

Parry, Adam. *The Making of Homeric Verse*. Oxford: Oxford University Press, 1971.

Post, L. A. "Moral Patterns in Homer." *Transactions of the American Philological Association* 70: 158–90.

Stanford, W. B., ed. *Odyssey*. London : Macmillan, 1965.

West, M. L., ed. *Hesiod, Theogony*. Oxford : Oxford University Press, 1966.

Whitman, Cedric. *Homer and the Heroic Tradition*. Cambridge, Mass. : Harvard University Press, 1958.

Woodhouse, W. J.. *Composition of Homer's Odyssey*. Oxford : Clarendon Press, 1930.

(Ancient texts cited or referred to will appear in the General Index under author's name, followed by the title of the specific work and the most commonly accepted method of reference to the pasage in question. Passages of the *Iliad* and *Odyssey* cited or referred to in the text or notes will be enumerated in a special index arranged by the order of the books in each work.)

Index

Because of the great frequency with which they occur, the following items are *not* indexed for the entire book: **Odysseus, Odyssey, Iliad, Telemachus, Penelope.** The same is true, in given chapters, where the items are the major subject(s) of the chapter in question: in ch. 1, **Cyclops**; in ch. 3, **Suitor(s)**; in ch. 4, **bard, Demodocus, Phemius.** In addition, proper names of epic characters mentioned in passing in passages directly quoted from epic or in footnotes are *not* indexed. An index of passages from the *Iliad* and *Odyssey* quoted or referred to in the text is given following the alphabetical index. To avoid a plethora of "ff." and *"passim"* in the index, where the item is referred to over several sequential pages, only the first page of the reference is indexed.

Index of Epic Passages